CoTeaching
Students with Autism
K–5

Judi Kinney and Debbie Fischer

IEP
RESOURCES

Authors: *Judi Kinney*   *Debbie Fischer*

Editor: *Tom Kinney*

Graphic Design: *Jo Reynolds*

Cover photo courtesy Gerald and Susan Brabender

ISBN: 1-57861-125-3

AN IEP RESOURCES PUBLICATION

P.O. BOX 930160   VERONA, WI 53593-0160

PHONE: 800-651-0954   FAX: 608-845-8040

Table of Contents

This book is dedicated to Sammy Jo,
my first student with autism, and a delightful young
woman who taught me how to grow as a teacher.
More than anyone, she is the inspiration for this book.

Acknowledgements

A special thanks to Sammy's family who helped me understand the uniqueness of the human body and the resiliency of the human spirit. To Susan, her mother, who made all of those Academy Award-winning Halloween costumes and kept us laughing through some hard moments with her wonderful stories about Sammy. To the men in her life: Her father, Jerry, whose heart is as big as he is tall and the touching way he spoke to his daughter; and Dustin, her older brother who patiently taught Sammy the social and dress rules of her peers and whose brotherly affection was evident. This family's support helped me realize that beyond the challenges, there are great joys that families with children with autism face.

My thanks also to Lee Wilder, who contributed frank and insightful thoughts and photos of her beautiful children to the parent chapter.

Many times I mention in this book that it takes an entire school to educate a child. Every special education teacher knows that the support of your IEP team is invaluable when searching for the formula for success for a child. Thanks to all the OT/PT staff who helped me achieve new dimensions in teaching and who patiently explained techniques for teaching children with unusual nervous systems and willingly gave their time and devotion to the many children in my program. To Carol Wilson who set up a Circle of Friends program for Sammy and Connie Maksymo who spent hours writing social stories. To Susie Berg who willingly took on the challenge and joy of educating many of the children discussed in this book and helped to expand their knowledge the following year.

A very special thank you to Nancy Bogucki a devoted child advocate and educational assistant. Nancy went well beyond her prescribed duties and it was her devotion that helped to put together the best possible program for Sammy. To Jill Larson, Mary Benjamin and Rebecca Studinski, important members of the special education program whose wisdom and friendship were invaluable.

Judi Kinney

Without a loving and supportive family,
I couldn't have continued in my career with the
dedication that it requires. Ron, Kari and Emily,
I thank you for your support, patience and love.

Acknowledgements

Throughout my career, I've had the good fortune to be surrounded by
creative and supportive teachers, dedicated parents and children eager
to learn. I've had the opportunity to attend many conferences and
read a number of professional books by prominent authors in my field.
All these factors have contributed to the successes I've had as a teacher
and I'm grateful for all of these influences on my career.

Debbie Fischer

Introduction

The current emphasis on an inclusion prototype for teaching students with special needs in the general education classroom has sent educators scurrying to find a model which can benefit children and best educate them.

When our school district decided to adopt an "inclusion model," teachers were told to "just do it!" While we have a capable and conscientious administration, no guidelines were given to us on how to do it and everyone had their own ideas as to what inclusion meant. With the passage of IDEA '97 more and more educators are finding themselves in this position: Suddenly asked to work with even the most challenging special needs students in an inclusion setting with little or no guidance.

Make no mistake, however, inclusion does work. It must! Students who have an educational handicap have the same rights to the best education possible, and should have the same access to the curriculum as the general population. Over the years of teaching together, often by trial and error, sometimes using an idea gleaned from an article, but mostly relying on a growing respect and trust for each other, Debbie and I have developed a model that has been successful. Together, we have taught students with learning and emotional disabilities, children identified as having other health impairments and students with autism.

While children with autism presented a unique challenge to us, they have also taught us how to be better teachers. Unfortunately, too often these students are being placed in general education classrooms without either teacher benefiting from appropriate inservicing. As a result teachers are often left to dig frantically for information and to try and figure out by themselves the best educational plan for these children.

We have had the privilege of teaching children who have been identified with Asperger Syndrome, Pervasive Developmental Delay and autism. Each child has been an individual, each has come with his or her own educational challenges, parental concerns and unique talents.

The model presented in this book is not a full inclusion one and coteaching did not take place all day long. Being a multicategorical LD/ED teacher I did not have the luxury of being assigned to only one classroom or one grade level.

> With the passage of IDEA '97, more and more educators suddenly are being asked to work with even the most challenging special needs students in an inclusive setting with little or no guidance.

From talking to other special educators, most teachers are in my position. How do you include a child when the specialists cannot be in the room for the entire school day? And from Debbie's perspective, how do you include a student with unique needs and challenging behaviors when the special education teacher is not always there to help?

It has been our experience that you must educate yourself as quickly as possible. Read, attend conferences, talk to competent colleagues, talk to parents and enlist the speech and language therapist and occupational and physical therapy departments. If it takes a village to raise a child, it takes a team of educators to instruct one.

This book is our attempt to impart some of these ideas to you. It does not attempt to be definitive or comprehensive, we'll leave that up to you. It's our contention that most teachers are: A, extremely capable, and B, operate in a unique environment all its own, with its own challenges suggesting their own solutions. This is simply an effort to present some approaches that have worked for us which you are free to use as is or adapt to your own purposes.

Judi Kinney

Profiles In Teaching

Judi Kinney

Special Education Teacher

While tracing my teaching trajectory over the years, I pondered things I hadn't thought about for a very long time. My journey takes several decades and I've seen many changes in the field of special education since the 1970s.

When I was an adolescent I had several incredible teachers who inspired me and I often thought about teaching as a career. But by the time I was in college—learning to love the freedom of a life without bells—I decided it was not for me.

One of the subjects I had a passion for—and still do—was history: Learning about humankind's endless conflicts while keeping in mind the ultimate resiliency of the human spirit. (Perhaps because it's the same resiliency I see everyday in my classrooms.) My first degree was in Russian/American History. However, I soon realized that in the real world a degree in history doesn't do much for your employability.

In the early 70's I found a job as a workshop coordinator in an institution for adults with cognitive and emotional disabilities. The residents of this nine-story building taught me a great deal during the time I worked there. (More often they were referred to as "patients," though most were quite hardy, or "kids," though the average age was late thirties, early forties.) Their stories were in turn fascinating and frustrating. The worst part was the locked ward where many residents walked on tiptoe, echoing everything that was said to them or that they heard from the omnipresent TV in the "dayroom," and screaming whenever a loud noise was made as they struggled to verbally communicate their needs. The "staff" consisted mostly of minimum wage nonprofessionals with the exception of the occasional "nurse" who was there to administer "meds," or give a "shot" to a disruptive resident, though the causes for their distress were usually preventable. The nurses were almost always two-year LPNs, rather than the more skilled and better trained RNs.

Meanwhile, the residents were allowed to engage in the most exotic behavior imaginable as long as it didn't interrupt the

> In order to help the students learn appropriate behaviors, I spent hours designing and redesigning point systems, behavior contracts and reinforcement hierarchies. The goal was to decrease inappropriate behaviors and increase socially acceptable ones. It didn't take long to discover that these students were far more complicated than any garden-variety behavior modification plan could cover.

When I worked at the institution, two leading theorists, Leo Kanner and Bruno Bettleheim, taught that autism resulted from the lack of a mother's nurturing (not the father's, of course) and had no neurological basis. The hideous phrase they coined was "refrigerator mom."

We regularly saw mothers (the few whose children had been properly diagnosed) come into the institution to visit their children. You could see the shame in their eyes from years of being told their child's autism was their fault. This was the first time I realized that parents aren't always responsible for their child's behavior or condition, a notion that also had currency in those days, and unfortunately still does among many professionals, including those in education.

peaceful and lucrative running of the institution, which was privately owned. Hand-flapping, perseverating, or "stimming" on a string dangled in front of a blank face, pacing, body rocking or making nonsense sounds—all were permitted. To interrupt these routines was to invite a violent episode.

This would seem to imply they were all people with autism. They weren't, of course, but in looking back I realize many were. Autism was less frequently diagnosed in those days. It was thought to be incurable and lifelong, a good reason to surrender your child at birth to the institutional system, often under the advice of the family doctor. So if your child was extremely involved and seemed to be developmentally disabled, a diagnosis of autism was considered irrelevant. I often wonder how many of the undiagnosed adults in that institution were people with autism who were potentially high functioning and could have had nearly normal lives had they not been institutionalized. That is, if they had been raised in a loving home environment and given an appropriate education.

As the workshop coordinator, finding employment for adults who'd only known institutional life was challenging. They'd had too little education, too little guidance of any kind, and a lot of time to develop aversive behaviors. The lost talent and wasted creativity in that building was overwhelming. I soon found myself back in graduate school at the University of Wisconsin majoring in special education . . . and I've been doing it ever since.

I entered teaching shortly after the passage of Chapter 89 in Wisconsin and when the first attempts to implement PL 94-142 had just begun. Although I did four student teaching practicums (one in regular education) and received a license in three disability categories, in my first twenty years of teaching I didn't encounter one student who was diagnosed with autism. At that time, most of these students were being shuttled into "severely disabled" classrooms or still continued to be institutionalized.

Instead, my attention turned to students with emotional disabilities. My first teaching experience was in a small community and I started the first ED Classroom ever taught in their junior high. Until the passage of PL 94-142, these children were expelled or suspended so often they frequently dropped out by default. Of all the disabilities this is the one the school community most often tends to blame on the child and parents. My task was to convince the regular educators and administration that these students were creative and intelligent children worthy of the attention they needed and so often craved. Needless to say that idea met with thunderous resistance.

In order to help the students learn appropriate behaviors, I spent hours designing and redesigning point systems, behavior contracts and reinforcement hierarchies. The goal was to decrease inappropriate behaviors and increase socially acceptable ones. It didn't take long to discover that these students were far more complicated than any garden-variety behavior modification plan could cover. I was uneasy when the eighth graders who graduated and enrolled in high school started to again exhibit behaviors that had long been extinguished in the junior high. A problem with those early, but well-meaning behavior programs was that they failed to teach students how to manage their own behavior and not just to respond to point systems. Needless to say, working with students with emotional and behavioral problems would come in handy later when I met my first students with autism.

Two years later I transferred to another junior high in yet a smaller community. Again, I was in charge of a brand new program for students with behavior problems. Here, my classroom was the first multicategorical one in the state. I taught students with learning disabilities and emotional problems. My room was a self-contained, integrated program which meant that except for study hall, language arts and mathematics, my students were in the regular education classrooms. At that time, neither special education teachers nor educational assistants were ever allowed to assist in a general education program.

It required me to be accessible. A common complaint then (and now) was that special education teachers never get enough prep time. Most of mine was spent in M-Team and IEP meetings, or to conference with administrators and general education teachers about children who broke the consensus rules for how students learn. It wasn't easy because everyone was still trying to interpret and follow the guidelines set by PL 94-142.

Questions constantly arose such as, who was responsible for the overall educational program of special education students, who was responsible for their discipline, and who held parent conferences?

It was the discipline part that was most often overwhelming. As the sole special education teacher, I was expected to do all the disciplining of the students even when they acted out in another teacher's classroom. This often meant detentions at noon hour or after school. Some days I thought I might as well have a foldout cot in my classroom closet, because there wasn't much point in going home that late in the day. Other days I wondered if I wasn't

> It was the discipline part that was most often overwhelming. As the sole special education teacher, I was expected to do all the disciplining of the students even when they acted out in another teacher's classroom.

> As much as I loved teaching, I couldn't be both educator and prison warden. Constantly sending kids to the special education room for missed assignments or bad behaviors, as a form of discipline, created a deficit model for educating children.

the one serving the detention, since the child who was being disciplined changed but I was always there.

As much as I loved teaching, I couldn't be both educator and prison warden. Constantly sending kids to the special education room for missed assignments or bad behaviors, as a form of discipline, created a deficit model for educating children. And it certainly wasn't a very creative approach. So, it became necessary to prevent these problems rather than just reacting to them.

In response, I mustered a handful of caring and dedicated teachers to help work on curriculum modifications such as study guides and study partners to help the students with academic concerns. And conferencing with teachers and students together served to reduce some of the acting out behaviors because it allowed the children to have some personal stake in their educational program.

Eventually I moved to an elementary classroom in the same district. Developing a team effort remained a priority. The onus for keeping the doors open for communication must fall on the special education teacher. A mistake I still see all the time is special educators sending their EAs to the general education classroom but seldom going themselves. Face-to-face contact is a necessity. Building relationships and trust by supporting teachers and parents is a must for a special education program to work.

By the time I left this small community, I had learned how to be a better teacher. I had taught children with learning disabilities, kids who were suicidal, who had been diagnosed with chronic allergies, with emotional and behavioral disorders, Tourette's Syndrome, conduct disorders, and attention deficit disorders. All along the way I made friends with staff and parents. But I still had not seen a single student with autism. And this was more than a decade after the passage of 94-142.

My next stint was as a preceptor in the special education department at the University of Wisconsin. As such I taught a special education methods and assessment class and I supervised student teachers at their practicum sites. Teaching new teachers was exciting and I was able to visit many classrooms and experience different instructional models.

At the university, a short lecture or overview was given on how to teach students with autism. Actually, we devoted about a half hour per semester. Unless a student teacher requested it, most student teachers were given little information on how to instruct this population. At the time, programs which served LD and ED students had few if any students with autism.

Missing the classroom and the children, I left the University after a half dozen years to return to the public schools. Over the past decade it has been my good fortune to teach in an elementary school with a highly competent staff. The creative genius found in many classrooms is exciting especially at a time when educators are trying to meet increased public expectations.

In my opinion, this is an electrifying time to teach. From a special educator's point of view, increased inclusion is slowly but inexorably dissolving the barriers between regular and special education. Unfortunately, but predictably, inclusion has brought with it a set of new problems and challenges. In our district, one change has been the rapidly increasing population of children with autism who are now sitting in many grade level classrooms.

Now, many years after my beginnings in this field, I am seeing a younger version of the institutionalized adults I worked with entering our schools. And while we still have a long way to go, it's a whole different world. With an early diagnosis, support from a stable home environment and appropriate education—in an inclusive setting as much as possible—children with autism have a real shot at a happy and productive life.

While in my first twenty years of teaching I had almost no contact with students with autism, in the past five years I've never had less than two on my class list at any time. Debbie has had almost every one of these students in her classroom. It has been my good fortune to have a colleague and friend who was as willing as I to learn about these unique and often gifted students.

While in my first twenty years of teaching I had almost no contact with students with autism, in the past five years I've never had less than two on my class list at any time. Debbie has had almost every one of these students in her classroom.

Profiles In Teaching

Debbie Fischer

Regular Education Teacher

It isn't entirely clear to me why I decided to become a classroom teacher, but I do remember a moment when the idea first occurred to me. I was 13 years old, sitting in a study hall and my eyes wandered across the hall in the direction of an elementary classroom, where they came to rest on an especially creative bulletin board. It hung right outside the room of a teacher I had always greatly admired for the myriad ways she had of engaging students in their work.

For some reason, bulletin board displays always caught my attention, and this one seemed so welcoming, such a positive message and so kid-friendly. This may have been the first time the teaching profession beckoned to me.

Years later, when discussing career path options with my chemistry teacher, I told him of my interests, which included among other things, laboratory work. He suggested I pick a career that involved being with people and encouraged me to pursue a teaching profession.

When the time came to choose a college, and subsequently the direction I would take once I arrived at the school of my choice, I always felt the pull of the teaching professions. Almost 30 years later I feel my original affinity for teaching and I continue to savor the time I spend with my students.

I graduated one late December from the University of Wisconsin-Whitewater. In the frozen northern midwest, it wasn't exactly the best time to land a good teaching job. But eventually I was hired as a substitute in a large metropolitan district. Shortly after, I was hired as a long-term kindergarten substitute in an elementary school that integrated hearing impaired children. From day one at that school children with disabilities were mainstreamed into my classroom. The school favored an approach known as the "total communication method," which required students to read lips using a minimum of sign language.

While I'd had no formal preparation for working with students with disabilities, my career essentially began in an inclusionary setting and I soon came to believe this was the way to teach all children. I have only grown more resolute in that belief in the decades since.

My next job was as a fully contracted first grade teacher in the same school and I never had less than one or two children with disabilities in my room. I became an advocate for these students and I came to support their parents as well. It was a strong program in a competent district and as I taught there over the years I saw peers and staff come to accept and understand children with disabilities and it made me feel good about the education we were able to provide.

After our first daughter was born, I resigned from my teaching position, and when three years later our second child came along, I continued to stay at home. However, chalk dust still ran in my blood and I became active in the education department of our church and helped to implement some new programs. I was also an assistant pre-school teacher for two years. By the time our youngest was in first grade, I began substitute teaching in her district. The next year they hired me as a second grade teacher in a job sharing position. I had the best of both worlds: Once again I was teaching, I still had time at home, and our girls were able to come to my classroom at the end of their school day.

This is in the district I still live and teach in.

I have now taught here for the past 13 years and counting, during which the ever-increasing inclusion of special education students in the regular education classroom continues to be a critical part of our educational programming. Rarely has a year gone by when I haven't had kids with disabilities in my room. I have partnered with special education teachers to work with children who are learning disabled, emotionally disturbed, cognitively challenged and autistic.

Over the past six years I've cotaught with special education teacher, Judi Kinney, coauthor of this book. During that time, we've developed a system that has been very successful for us, for our school and for the kids with special needs in our classes. It is because we've had that period of time to fine-tune our strategies that they work so well.

As for the children in our classes, I regard each and every one of them as an individual, and as I teach I think about what it feels like to be a parent. I try my level best to offer quality education to all of them.

As for the future, I will continue to take post-graduate courses and read as many professional journals and research findings as I can to keep up with the latest ideas and educational theory in order to provide a sound education for all my students.

While it's not always clear to me why I chose this profession, what is clear is why I stay in it: For those shining faces that enter my room with a mixture of expectation, excitement and anxiety each year and leave with a feeling of accomplishment, connection to the system, and anticipation for their future at the end of each year.

Over the past six years I've cotaught with special education teacher, Judi Kinney, coauthor of this book. During that time, we've developed a system that has been very successful for us, for our school and for the kids with special needs in our classes. It is because we've had that period of time to fine-tune our strategies that they work so well.

Chapter One

CoTeaching—
It Can Work

Cooperation between special education teachers and general education teachers concerning students in grade level classes is not new. In the past, mainstreaming special education students has meant that part of their school day was spent in general education classrooms. Some special education teachers and/or educational assistants accompanied these students into the classrooms and helped to assist according to the rules laid out by the general educator. The role most often assumed by the special education teacher was that of a glorified aide or parent volunteer. Rarely was there an opportunity to share the teaching.

Unfortunately, in too many districts, inclusion continues to mean that special needs students are dumped on general education staff with minimal support from administration, inadequate training and not enough face-to-face contact between the regular and special education teachers in an inclusive setting.

Special education students are in these classes for various reasons. Probably the most important one is that many parents of children with special needs are concerned with the amount of "pull-out" that is occurring with their child. In fact, almost from the beginning of special education, as we know it today, parents have fought to have their children mainstreamed.

Furthermore the passage of IDEA '97 has only increased the pressure to keep these students in the general education classrooms. Parents, students, and administrators are insisting that special education students obtain the same access to the general curriculum as other students. In many, if not most districts, an inclusion model has replaced the old mainstreaming concept. When implemented effectively, this does not seem to be an unreasonable approach. And it seems to be an inevitable transition.

However, any time there's a major paradigm shift in the way we do things, questions naturally arise. Some include:

⁂ How can inclusion occur so that all children benefit?

> In the past, the role most often assumed by the special education teacher was that of a glorified aide or parent volunteer. Rarely was there an opportunity to share the teaching.

- How do general and special educators decide how to share responsibilities?
- Which (if either) of the two teachers should take the lead?
- What type and how much inservice is needed?
- How are disruptive behaviors dealt with and are they the sole responsibility of the special educator?
- Should the special educator work with the general education students in the class as well?
- Should the general educator work with special needs students?
- Are all students to be included, no matter what their individual behavioral or academic needs?
- Why are some special educators, who clearly feel uncomfortable about inclusion, allowed to continue pull-out programs?
- How do you deal with general educators who are resistant to inclusion and constantly seek to sabotage it?
- How are inclusion and coteaching implemented in smaller districts where there are limited resources?

This is a very short list of questions and concerns that educators throughout the country have wrestled with since the passage of IDEA '97.

Unfortunately, in many districts teachers have been left to scramble to design an inclusive educational program which works and which they themselves have had to develop. In the past, our district had set aside inservice money to present current and important topics to the entire teaching staff. However, with the anticipation of the passage of IDEA '97, "include" came down to us as an edict from the administrative staff.

> With inclusion, a significant change in teaching roles had taken place. Yet, there was no additional money, inservicing, guidelines or models presented to instructional and support staff.

In their definition of inclusion it was implied that there would be some coteaching because it was envisioned that the special educator would spend more time with students in the general education classrooms. This meant, of course, that a significant change in teaching roles had taken place. Yet, there was no additional money, inservicing, guidelines or models presented to the teaching and support staff. Apparently what happened in our district was not unusual. In the initial stage it depended upon the skills of the individual general and special education teachers to make inclusion and coteaching work. As a result, for awhile some classroom teachers had adapted an inclusion model, some were willing to try coteaching and others insisted that the more traditional pull-out program take place or that the role of the special education teacher remain one of an assistant. There was a gap between reality and the law. In speaking with other special education teachers from surrounding districts, the scramble to make inclusion a part of coteaching has been similar to what has occurred in our district.

The inclusion and coteaching model in Debbie's classroom was one that was slowly developed over time. It depended upon the chemistry, trust, and philosophies which meshed nicely between the two of us. The program works because it evolved slowly with much trial and error experimentation and lots of fine tuning. Behind that was our belief that the education of the students was more important than a rush job to comply with a coteaching philosophy. As our approach started to take form, parents of special needs kids for the most part became allies and supported our efforts to design a classroom structure that educated all.

How much coteaching should you do?

It depends on a number of factors:

* ✹ How many students the special educator has on her caseload.

* ✹ How many different places she has to be during the day.

* ✹ The commitment of your district to inclusion and coteaching.

* ✹ The resources your district has to invest in an inclusion and coteaching model.

We don't coteach all day, only a part of it. Judi doesn't have the time. She has too many students in too many places to spend the entire day in Debbie's room. That may or may not be your situation.

If you are coteaching part of the day, optimize your time by looking at your schedules and deciding which periods are best to begin with. For example, the first year we taught together, when we were still finding our way, Debbie had students with learning disabilities and other health impaired in her class. So Judi was in there for language arts programming. Language arts and math are the two major areas of concern for special needs students and for their parents. These would be our two top choices to start with, since they represent an academic area that is essential for the student to be supported in and is crucial to his or her academic advancement. Most parents would support you completely on this prioritization.

> We don't coteach all day, only a part of it. Judi doesn't have the time. She has too many students in too many places to spend the entire day in Debbie's room. That may or may not be your situation.

> Students who were in Debbie's room for language arts and had additional pull-out time with Judi did extremely well on our statewide reading tests.

When we began inclusion at our school, a whole language program had recently been implemented. At this time, our reading specialist began tracking students who had significant reading difficulties to be sure that inclusion along with a whole language approach was meeting their needs. Several years later our reading specialist had data which indicated that students who were in Debbie's room for language arts and also had some additional pull-out time with Judi for learning specific skills did extremely well on our statewide reading tests. We think there were two reasons for these positive results:

1. The special needs students in Debbie's language arts classes heard good reading models on a consistent basis.

2. Being in the regular education classroom, despite their difficulties, gave them confidence in their abilities to handle the reading materials. With additional pull-outs to strengthen their skills, they showed superior abilities to their peers who were exclusively in pull-outs.

And then along came Maria

The end result of many hours of planning, working, and learning together had just started to take shape when in walked Maria, a beautiful child, who on the first day of school stood outside the classroom and repeated over and over, "Will it hurt her? Will it hurt her?" Maria was the first of many students who were to be educated in our classroom who had been diagnosed with autism or pervasive developmental delay. We realized immediately that a unique challenge was being presented to us.

Like it was with inclusion, when children with autism first started to come to our district there was very little money set aside to educate teachers as to how to best instruct these very challenging but creative children. In all fairness to the administration, the number of students with this disability that eventually enrolled in the district took everyone off guard.

What it meant was that now the teaching and support staff had to not only struggle with inclusion and coteaching, but also we had to learn how to best educate students with autism, all of whom were as different from each other as possible.

So, an additional set of questions arose:

※ What basic skills did we need to work with children with autism?

※ Where could parents get support?

✳ Does inclusion also mean that support staff, such as speech and language and OT/PT, should come into the general classroom?

✳ How often is it necessary to have outside consultants' view the classroom and meet with the IEP team?

✳ How do you cope with the often intense advocacy that parents of kids with autism bring in the door?

✳ What is the role of outside consultants brought in by parent advocacy groups?

The purpose of this book is to talk about the issues surrounding inclusion, coteaching and how to educate children who presented a different kind of social and academic challenge. We will share our experiences and best methods for developing a coteaching plan for children with pervasive developmental delay and autism. Our situation is not unique but we hope that others can benefit from it.

The origins of our program

When we started to work together neither of us knew much about the other. Initially, when Judi came into the classroom her role was little more than that of the EA. The old mainstreaming concept was still the model that guided us. Fortunately, Debbie brought a lengthy experience in working with kids with special needs to the table. In addition, Judi was a veteran special education teacher who was certified in all disability areas.

Together, it didn't take us long to discover that we were a powerful team if we planned out our day carefully and openly shared our concerns and ideas about coteaching special education students in the general classroom . . . and most importantly, if we continued to adjust and adapt our approach as we learned. At first we needed weekly planning sessions to tweak our evolving program and in the course of these discovered that we had similar philosophies about educating children, similar ideas on discipline procedures, and finally that we were willing and eager to share teaching responsibilities.

Although our goal was to have special education students in the general classroom for the entire day we built enough flexibility in the schedule to handle academic and behavior problems as they arose. However, the coteaching model that developed was not one that saw us both in a single classroom all day long. Judi had too many students in other classes to have that luxury.

Although our goal was to have special education students in the general classroom for the entire day, we built enough flexibility in the schedule to handle academic and behavior problems as they arose.

BRIGHT IDEA!

> A common concern among many special educators in coteaching relationships is that they are under-used. General education teachers, you have a highly trained, skilled coworker in your room . . . why not make the most of her?

Other factors in a successful coteaching situation include:

* **Style and substance**—in order to develop a good professional relationship one needs to know the other person's style of teaching and disciplining. In our situation we both were veteran teachers and felt confident with our teaching methods. A similar length of time in the classroom could be part of the reason why our coteaching style worked. While both of us were impressed with the other's credentials and abilities, neither of us were intimidated by our coteacher. When suggestions were made or ideas presented neither felt the other was invading her territory. We were both eager to share.

* **The "co" in coteaching**—some general educators enjoy having an additional body in their room but continue to delegate teacher responsibilities as they did before coteaching became an educational model. A common concern among many special educators in coteaching relationships is that they feel under-used. General education teachers, you have a highly trained, skilled coworker in your room . . . why not make the most of her?

* **Changing roles**—inclusion means a shift in roles for both the special and general education teachers. For the special educator, despite your training and your instincts, you have to learn to place less emphasis on specific skills and more on helping the student fit into the pace of large group learning without too much loss of academic ground. Behavioral and disciplining issues become paramount in this setting. Remember, academic skills can be strengthened in pull-outs so students continue to be successful in the large group setting. The regular educator has to learn to view her classroom as a place where two teachers work side by side.

* **Watch your language**—we both have similar ways of thinking about, and as a result, talking about our students. We appreciate and enjoy their talents as well as their idiosyncrasies; the things that make an individual an individual. It's easy to look at the deficits special education students have. Sometimes they're easier to see than their strengths. Teacher language helps set an atmosphere for learning. The next time you're in the teacher's lounge, listen carefully. How often have you heard otherwise caring teachers saying something about the "LDs", the "low-lows," or "the autistics" in their classrooms? How often have you heard the expression "the good kids" used almost as a code

word for students who are not in special education. In today's multicultural classrooms children with special education needs are too often referred to by their labels rather than their names. We were both committed to viewing all students as having academic/social abilities rather than weaknesses.

✖ **Challenge each other**—we both had strong personalities and definite opinions, but this was one of the key strengths in our working relationship. We thrived on the challenges each of us could present to the other.

✖ **The right stuff**—Debbie not only enjoyed challenges from colleagues, she also was willing to teach some of the most difficult students entering her grade. As a result we were able to teach year after year with each other because many of those students were on Judi's caseload.

✖ **It takes time**—a must for developing a coteaching classroom is the opportunity to work with each other for an extended period of time. A team cannot grow strong unless there's the opportunity to teach from year to year. Many of the support staff people and parents saw our teaching relationship as an opportunity for children to learn and grow. Their opinion helped to give validity to what we were attempting to do.

✖ **Keep current**—we're both committed to learning new information. We're avid readers and we shared articles, videos and conference information with each other. This compulsion of ours to keep current really paid off when students with autism were first introduced into our classroom. Debbie made a point of purchasing topical professional materials, often out of her own pocket. Judi kept a small library of videos and books in her room to share with anyone who wanted more information. When the opportunity arose for Judi to join a teacher's writer's workshop that was started by Debbie and a middle school teacher, she did it. The workshop gave a forum to discuss good teaching practices.

Teachers need to constantly read the professional material being published. No one wants to have surgery done by a physician who has not kept up with the latest procedures.

BRIGHT IDEA!

The special education teacher must develop credibility as a reliable classroom ally. It's the regular educator's classroom. Before you can share it, you have to prove you belong there.

Judi

The initial role of the special education teacher

※ **Earn your credibility**—before trying to develop a coteaching model the special education teacher must develop credibility as a reliable classroom ally. Pay your dues. Don't take anything for granted. It's her classroom. Before you can share it, you have to prove you belong there.

※ **Communicate on basics**—use your common sense: For example, a major complaint, in speaking with general educators from other districts, is that too often educational assistants are sent into the general classroom when the teacher was expecting the special education teacher. That's not to say there wasn't a good reason for it. Meetings and crisis situations can and will interfere with a special education teacher's daily schedule. And the nature of a crisis is that it comes out of nowhere. Nonetheless, it's a must that the regular education instructor knows why a change has been made. If you can't forewarn her, at least tell her as soon afterwards as you can.

※ **Extra instruction**—you need a solid and consistent plan for extra small group instruction to help students who are struggling academically. Write your IEPs to allow for this flexibility. Special education instructor's schedules have always been difficult and inclusion has made it even more so. Consider pulling students as soon as they arrive at school and work on problematic academic concepts during the grade level leisure reading block.

※ **Discipline and behavior management**—a plan for removing students or handling disruptive behavior is a must. In talking with teachers of all disciplines this is almost always their most pressing concern. Some children with autism can become physically abusive. You need a carefully written functional behavioral program to deal with them without hesitation. And share the plan with your coteacher. That allows frustrated children to be redirected or removed with dignity and keeps the general educator from feeling alone when the special educator is not in the room.

※ **Become familiar with the curriculum**—sometimes bedtime reading is a necessity. You must have a grasp of the entire regular education curriculum to be able to support your students.

- **Communicate appreciation**—let the classroom teacher know when she's done a really great job . . . the way she answered a student question, or a lesson plan that peaked student interest. How often do teachers go without reinforcement for their efforts?
- **Keep your opinions to yourself**—don't openly judge regular education teachers in front of their peers or the special education staff. There are channels to express concerns. The rumor and gossip mill is not one of them. Approach her one-on-one, if necessary.
- **Don't get in the way**—when you're not teaching, stay out of the lines of communication between the students and your coteacher. You are moveable, most of the time the students are not.
- **Don't hover**—unless there is a safety issue do not hover over the special education students. You might just as well be standing there with a giant arrow that says, "problem child."
- **Compliment all student work and behavior**—as you walk about the classroom, let (all) students know when their work and behavior is exemplary. Do it in a quiet manner so the flow of instruction is not interrupted. Even the best general education teachers don't always have time to do this. The students will start to value your opinion and see you as an important part of the classroom.
- **Evolve relationships**—try to eat regularly with the teachers with whom you most closely work. This is one of the few times in the day when you have the opportunity to learn about each other's personal life.
- **Be prepared**—bring a notebook with you to the general education classroom to jot down concerns about schedules, homework assignments, project due dates, specific skills your students need to be successful and questions to ask parents. (See example, pg. 31.)
- **Meeting times**—find mutually agreed upon meeting times to plan schedules with your coteacher.
- **Communicate successes and struggles**—keep open lines of communication with the classroom teacher about students who are having difficulties as well as those who appear to be mastering the content.
- **Rotate meetings**—don't always hold meetings in just one

Unless there is a safety issue, don't hover over the special education students. You might just as well be standing there with a giant arrow that says, "problem child."

BRIGHT IDEA!

Reproducible:

See pg. 31 for a form to jot down concerns about schedules, homework assignments, project due dates, specific skills your students need to be successful and questions to ask parents.

room. Balance additional meetings between the class and resource rooms. Teachers can then become familiar with each other's home base.

⁜ **Ask questions**—communicate clearly when in doubt about anything.

⁜ **Develop a sub plan**—have a fallback plan that will enable a substitute teacher (both regular and special) to walk into the classroom and make a clean transition. (A reproducible is available on pg. 33.)

Debbie

The initial role of the general educator

⁜ **Have confidence**—be comfortable with yourself and your teaching style. When another teacher enters your classroom it's difficult to be effective if you're constantly second guessing yourself.

⁜ **Be realistic**—you will make mistakes and you won't know all of the answers, but that shouldn't stop you from working hard at giving your students your best shot.

⁜ **Introduce your coteacher**—it's important to introduce your coteacher as soon as possible, making sure you don't identify her as the "special ed" teacher. Nor should you ever single out any students who she is there to support. Judi is always introduced as another classroom teacher who is there to help us all, and all children are encouraged to ask her questions as freely as they ask me.

⁜ **Let your coteacher's strengths strengthen you**—Judi is knowledgeable in history and a committed gardener and naturalist. While I can't approach her grasp of history, gardening and nature, I can certainly defer to her on these subjects, thus benefiting both of us. So when discussions arise in these areas, we let our classroom "expert" take center stage. In fact, we often save questions until Judi comes into the room. She's always willing to share information and this has become another way in which we're a team that works together.

⁜ **Share the space**—respect each other's space and be aware of each other's body language. Judi and I are able to "work" the entire room, never tripping over each other and always serving everyone.

It's important to introduce your coteacher as soon as possible, making sure you don't identify her as the "special ed" teacher.

BRIGHT IDEA!

- **Listen and learn**—special education teachers are (or should be) experts in areas of discipline and behavior management. Take advantage of their expertise. Working with Judi has helped me grow as an educator. From the beginning of our coteaching work, I knew I would strengthen my teaching skills by learning from her. I welcome her comments and her wisdom.

Use your special educator as you would an outside consultant.

- **Make constant adjustments**—we brainstorm solutions for just about everything, either sharing successes or going back to the drawing board for another strategy. If you stay on top of it, you'll only get better. And since Judi is in and out of the classroom, I need these strategies and knowledge to handle all kinds of situations when she's not there.

- **Make your coteacher feel comfortable**—regardless of whether the special education teacher is in your classroom all day or not, whenever she's there it's important for her to feel that it's "our" room. I never want her to feel she is stepping into my territory. We share a common space, and more importantly a common goal.

- **Share classroom instruction**—make sure your coteacher feels comfortable during planning time to teach anything she wants to the entire class. However, at the same time make sure she doesn't feel you're dumping on her. In our case, since Judi has a number of classrooms to rotate between, I don't want her overloaded with extra planning for a lesson in the regular education classroom. Share these determinations. In addition, we take turns leading classroom discussions and reading to the class as well as occasional small group projects.

- **Be flexible**—in the course of an average school day, the best plans can change ten times. More often than not we ended up with plan B, C, or D.

- **Be understanding**—in a "perfect" inclusion classroom the special and regular education teachers would work together all day, never having to worry about the rest of the classrooms. We've never had a perfect inclusion classroom. With the exception of some college-based experimental test courses, I suspect nobody does. In our district special education teachers are assigned to many classrooms and serve a number of children with very diverse needs. When Judi is called at the last minute because of a crisis situation in another room we both have to cope with it. Ideally, the entire school should function as a team with these shared understandings.

The entire school should function as a team with shared understandings.

Keep a folder handy for substitutes with special notes that include the teaching schedule and the role of the special education teacher in preventing misunderstandings. This is one great advantage of coteaching: When one is gone, the other can help the transition go smoothly.

BRIGHT IDEA!

Reproducibles:

See pg. 33–35 for a fallback plan that will enable substitute teachers (both regular and special) to walk into the classroom and make a clean transition.

※ **Keep your sense of humor**—without a sense of humor there are days that could drive you to tears. We try to help each other stay as lighthearted as possible.

※ **Stay organized**—whenever possible, stick to the schedule that you have laboriously preplanned together. It helps to make the unexpected incidents of the day easier to handle.

※ **Communicate constantly**—in addition to a scheduled planning time we talk as we walk down the hall, eat lunch, or walk to our cars. We also leave notes in each other's mailboxes or voice mail messages to update student progress or assignment results.

※ **Inform substitute teachers**—you don't want all your hard work to break down because you miss a day. Keep a folder handy for substitutes with special notes that include the teaching schedule and the role of the special education teacher in preventing misunderstandings. This is one great advantage of coteaching: When one is gone, the other can help the transition go smoothly.

※ **Learn your student's specific special needs**—use your special education coteacher's expertise to understand her students. That will make you be more effective in working with them. Sometimes it's helpful to read or view an educational video about a specific disability.

※ **Welcome comments about all students**—it's amazing what another set of eyes can see. Don't feel threatened when your coteacher points out something a special needs student might not have understood. Instead, be glad you caught it early.

※ **Keep a notebook handy**—we have a notebook that has been divided into sections for each student that's always on hand. Since it's not always possible for us to stop and talk, a quick note for your coteacher can be written down regarding any student. Don't miss any opportunity to communicate important information about your students.

※ **Enjoy each other**—share your friendship with the class. Let students see you work together and let them see that you share a friendship. A quick question about the progress of a flower garden or sharing the title of a good book can help spread the feeling of a community within the classroom.

Considerations once your coteaching program has been established:

✳ **Prepare for the lesson that you will teach.** Regular education students need to see that the special education teacher is as familiar with the topics as their classroom teacher. Special education students need to see that the regular education teacher understands their needs.

✳ **Mix special and regular education students in small group instruction.** Don't segregate by ability. Mixed groups allow the special education teacher to view the learning styles of many students and give the general education teacher an opportunity to observe the learning styles of special education students. This is especially important for students with autism who may have an educational assistant. It allows general educators to gain confidence in their ability to teach these challenging children and it encourages an additional relationship for the children with autism.

✳ **Be careful that students with autism who have a one-on-one assistant don't come to rely too heavily on them** as a third party interpreter.

✳ **Hold parent conferences together** in the grade level classroom. This helps communicate to all parents that the child with autism or pervasive developmental delay is as much a part of the class as every other child.

✳ **Have an occasional social gathering outside of school.** A dinner spent talking about personal interests can be relaxing and revealing.

✳ **Don't communicate problems or concerns shared in confidence**, especially between grade levels.

The model and techniques presented in this manual are an attempt to help other professionals who have had to find ways to include and coteach children with a variety of neurological, educational, and social needs.

(Note: pgs. 31–47 are reproducibles. They include: class notes, sub folder with filled out sample, class list, schools staff info, daily schedule with sample, and a weekly student schedule with sample.)

> Mixed groups are especially important for students with autism who have an educational assistant, because general educators gain confidence in their ability to teach them and it encourages additional relationships for these children.

Class Notes

Date _____

Notes

Assignments

Notes

Assignments

Notes

Assignments

Sub Folder Sample

Welcome:

Thank you for coming in to help teach a great group of students.
This is an inclusive program which means that you will be teaching students in the resource room as well as the regular education classroom. If you have questions, please feel free to ask the EAs or the students. All are very helpful.

Thank you—Judi Kinney

Explanation of Program:

This is a multi-categorical classroom, which means that the students have many unique learning and behavior problems. The children are in grades K—3. Please follow the schedule, as you will be in many different classrooms.

Some children come to the resource room for additional instruction. Each student has their own individual notebook in which lessons are written. The notebooks are in their assignment folders.

Please read the schedule. Please write comments about joys and concerns.

Contents of Folder:

A. **Class List** of students and their regular education teachers

B. **School Staff**—names of office staff and educational assistants

C. **Daily Schedule** (please feel free to remove and place on the clipboard)

D. **Other Information** such as the crisis procedure, health concerns and where classroom materials are located

Sub Folder

Welcome:

_____

_____

_____

_____

Explanation of Program:

_____

_____

_____

_____

_____

_____

_____

Contents of Folder:

A. **Class List** of students and their regular education teachers

B. **School Staff**—names of office staff and educational assistants

C. **Daily Schedule** (please feel free to remove and place on the clipboard)

D. **Other Information** such as the crisis procedure, health concerns and where classroom materials are located

Class List

Name	Grade	Classroom Teacher	Ext. No.	Room No.

School Staff

Title	Name	Ext. No.	Room No.
Principal			
Secretary			
Health Office			
Educational Assistants			
Other			

Crisis Procedure:

Medical Info:

Daily Schedule Sample

Date _3/28/01_   Staff _Judi Kinney_

Time	Schedule
7:45–8:15 *(Go to Mrs. Fischer's room)*	Power walk with Maria— (she likes to use the 1 lb. weights on her arms). While power walking practice her spelling words with her. (See individual assignment folder.) 8:01— Go to Maria's classroom— read the schedule to her. Assist her with the math journal, lunch count and calendar— Maria's job for the week is the calendar (see her classroom).
8:15–8:45 *(Math/Spelling in Mrs. Fischer's room)*	Help Maria use the Unifix cubes to do two math problems in her journal (the total amount should equal today's date.) Assist her in setting up the problems by dotting out the numbers she gives you to add. Maria can trace over the numbers. Maria's spelling words are in her notebook in her desk. Maria's EA arrives at 8:05.
8:45–9:15 *(Mrs. Berger's room)*	Go to Mrs. Berger's room— third grade (see class list for students in her room). The class is currently reading fairy tales. Today the students will be reading in partners. Please monitor the groups my students are in. Help all children who may have a question about the assignment.
9:15–9:45 *(Resource room)*	Students from Mrs. Berger's room come to the resource room to do a story map of the fairy tale they have just read. (see assignment folders.) Spelling group from Ms. McElver's room comes— see individual assignment notebook for lesson. Maria comes for reading assignment.
Comments	Please write comments here.

Daily Schedule

Date_____   Staff_____

Time	Schedule
Comments	

Weekly Student Schedule Sample

Teacher's Name _____Mrs. Fischer_____   Class/Grade _____Room 236_____

Student Name _____Charlie Smith_____   Week of _____3/26/01_____

	Monday	Tuesday	Wednesday	Thursday	Friday
8:00–8:30	lunch count classroom jobs math journal	→			→
8:30–9:00	Teacher of the day Chunking–chunk for this week is "ound"	→			→
9:00–9:30	spelling weekend news	spelling finish weekend news	spelling start reading Rosa Parks	spelling groups assigned writing organizer for Rosa Parks	spelling start writing on Rosa Parks
9:30–10:00	recess	→			→
10:00–10:30	R.E.A.D.time Charlie to resource room	→		Charlie's reading pod here	→
10:30–11:00	timed tests math–carry instruct digit nos.	timed tests	timed tests finish packets	timed tests start borrowing	timed tests →
11:00–11:30	lunch	→			→
11:30–12:00	11:15–Read aloud book art	music	P.E.	P.E.	sharing music
12:00–12:30					
12:30–1:00	unit on solids, liquids, gauges order solids	liquids, gauges weigh solids	discuss liquids notes taken	liquid experiment	compare liquids and solids
1:00–1:30	recess	→			→
1:30–2:00	worksheet on solids	computer lab	continue science report	Fourth grade orchestra concert	edit report for computer lab for next week
2:00–2:30	start science report	use science project continue report		↓	
2:30–3:00	check homeroom project				

Weekly Student Schedule

Teacher's Name _____ Class/Grade _____

Student Name _____ Week of _____

Time	Monday	Tuesday	Wednesday	Thursday	Friday

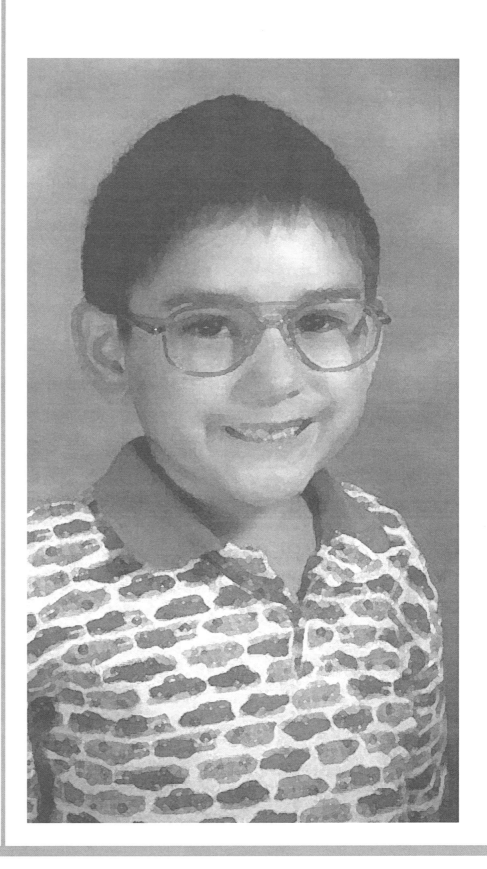

Chapter Two

Fall Trimester

Preparing for the school year

The first day, Debbie's room fills up like a champagne glass with bubbling, excited kids, animated conversation and students eagerly anticipating a new school year. Her room—which looks out on our arboretum—has a fenced-in area for large group instruction, shelves bulging with stuffed bears and buckets full to overflowing with books awaiting to be explored by young readers. It is, in short, a kid-friendly room. A safe haven for all children to learn.

However, the critical planning for students takes place long before that first day of school. The groundwork for the success of children with autism or pervasive developmental delay starts the preceding spring. We have discovered that when making transitional plans for children with autism, who seem to crave sameness, it's wise to prepare them carefully ahead of time for changes in their routine. Nothing is more threatening for them than a new school year, with new classes, new teachers, new everything.

So, each school year actually begins the spring before, when the first notices of class placements are presented at grade level meetings and tentative class lists are set. While placements remain subject to some change over the summer, at this point we have a good idea which special education students will be placed in Debbie's classroom and how difficult the challenge ahead of us will be.

Photo stories

When working with children with autism, who typically have a hard time adjusting to new environments, we take a series of digital photos each spring for the students and their families to study over the summer as a way of acclimating them to next year's class. Many are general in nature, e.g., welcome to your new classroom. However, they can also be specific to the student, e.g., a student who is fearful of the sound of a fire alarm could have her own photo story book of a fire drill to prepare for it.

> When making transitional plans for children with autism, who crave sameness, prepare them ahead of time for changes in their routine. Nothing is more threatening than a new school year, with new classes, new teachers, new everything.

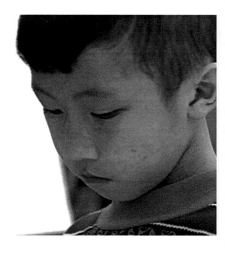

The following is an example of a photo story, presented in sequence. You can make your own photo book using pictures you take of your students with autism.

Going into a new grade

❋ A picture of this year's general education teacher waving goodbye from her classroom door.

❋ A picture of that teacher walking away down the hall.

❋ A picture of the student walking to his new classroom.

❋ A picture of next year's teacher smiling at the entrance of the student's new classroom and greeting the child.

❋ A picture of the student in the room.

❋ A picture of the room itself (There are some exceptions. For example, if we know the teacher but there's some doubt about the where the classroom will be, we will skip the picture of the room and just keep a closeup of the teacher greeting the child to avoid confusion.)

❋ If possible, a picture of a student from this year's class that will be in the same classroom next year to provide some continuity.

❋ A picture of the special education teacher and aide so that the student will know that there will be some familiar faces in that new classroom.

These pictures are placed on pages with a written script and made into a laminated book. Several copies are made and one is sent home for the family to read over the summer.

Other spring preparations:

❋ We make sure there's an opportunity for the families to visit Debbie's room and ask questions about the coming school year. Most families take this time to share their concerns and dreams for their child. This is not an IEP team meeting. At this time the parents can see the room, look at the curriculum and get acquainted with the general education teacher before the school year starts.

❋ IEP goals are shared and a copy given to Debbie so that both teachers are on the same page in the fall. If an IEP review was scheduled for the spring, Debbie attended that meeting as well as the previous grade level teacher. It gave her some

We make sure there's an opportunity for the families to visit Debbie's room and ask questions about the next school year.

BRIGHT IDEA!

information as to which approaches had been successful in the child's last general education classroom.

- The students are also invited to visit their next year's classroom in the spring. This is handled in a variety of ways, depending upon the needs of each child with autism. This is a sensitive matter and you should think it out carefully ahead of time. For example, one boy visited during silent reading time and seemed to be pleased he had a personal tour. But he tended to be more socially adept than some of the others. On the other hand, we knew that several other students with autism would be put off, possibly even mildly traumatized, by going into a class filled with strangers and staying for a silent reading period. We arranged for them to visit the room with an EA during a recess period so they could first become acquainted with the physical space that would be their next year's classroom. We also set it up so Debbie would be there to meet them and conduct their tour. It gave them a chance to see who their regular education teacher would be.
- Prior to the school year, once class lists are public and more or less set, we send out a form letter to students and their parents. It's very basic and gives us a starting point with each student. It gives parents a chance to express their goals and expectations. Each student also had an opportunity to respond to their own set of questions and could tell us something about himself. We recommend that a self addressed stamped envelope be sent to encourage a prompt reply. Students, on the other hand, could bring their questionnaires in on the first day of school.
- The combination of these steps: The sharing of information; meeting the parents, the students and their aides; and reviewing the IEP gave us both enough information to reflect over the summer as to the best approach for each student in the fall.

Meeting the students

Over the years of teaching students with autism or pervasive developmental delay, one factor stands out. These students are as different from each other as any other child in the classroom. If one approaches children with autism as teachable students with their own unique strengths, the task of instructing them becomes less insurmountable. Many people, including some professionals, cling to the old stereotype that these students are

Reproducibles:

See pgs. 59–61 for parent and student questionnaires.

After years of teaching students with autism, one factor stands out. These students are as different from each other as any other child in the classroom.

mostly nonverbal, cannot be taught social interactions, are "cold" and have minimal academic potential. It's important to note that not every child diagnosed with autism has a special education teacher or individual educational assistant. The children presented in the following pages—though challenging at times—possessed strengths and gifts, like any other child, and on occasion possessed talents that were quite extraordinary.

This manual follows the case studies of three hypothetical students with autism—who are based on rough composites of kids we've worked with—and looks at how their individual educational plan (IEP) was implemented over the course of an entire school year. They include students we've had with Asperger Syndrome, Pervasive Developmental Disorder, Childhood Disintegrative Disorder and Autism.

Just working from the medical diagnoses alone these children have a wide range of verbal, academic, and social needs. However, this book will not attempt to delve into the definitions put forth by the medical community. While as teachers these diagnoses can provide helpful guidelines for individual children, they do not necessarily translate into classroom instruction. Instead we will concentrate upon teaching techniques and modifications which we've implemented with the following composite students:

Charlie

Charlie was an attractive, quiet and gentle child who possessed many academic strengths. He was verbally fluent but not always able to use his language to communicate needs and ideas. In our experience, most of the students with autism or pervasive development disorders wanted to be part of the large group. And friendships seemed as important to them as they did to other kids. But for a variety of reasons, social connectedness often alluded them. Charlie struggled with social interactions and was not different from other children with autism in this respect.

If one approaches children with autism as teachable students with their own unique strengths, the task of instructing them becomes less insurmountable.

At first he seemed unable to respond to peer attempts to initiate conversations. The social rules for "study buddy" or small group learning situations were unclear and confusing to him. Because he was puzzled about how to respond verbally in the classroom, Charlie's academic strengths weren't able to shine through.

At least not in the beginning of the school year. As a result, recess time was spent wandering around from one piece of equipment to another. Sometimes he attempted to participate in group games, but here again for Charlie "social and game rules" were not easily grasped.

When he was able to engage in a game, Charlie preferred playing four square, since his poor gross motor skills appeared to interfere with the faster pace of soccer, football or basketball games. The rare times Charlie attempted to join a team game he was often picked last by the designated captain.

Charlie did have difficulty with body space issues. He shrank from children who tried to touch him. When large group instruction took place on the rug, Charlie had to sit on the outside of the group. If he found himself in the middle of the group he became so uncomfortable that he could not concentrate on the lesson being taught. He spent his time trying to find enough space about him so he did not feel crowded. As a result he bumped into his peers who generally weren't happy about being distracted.

Charlie's academic strengths included decoding skills, spelling and rote math concepts. If one heard Charlie reading aloud he sounded like any other reader in the class. His ability to decode individual words was impressive. If assigned to read with a buddy, Charlie was able to manage most of the words without assistance.

His shortcoming in this area was that he perceived written material only as a string of unconnected individual words. He didn't grasp the central purpose of a reading assignment, especially if the material was fiction. Important story elements, such as the main character, where the story took place, what actually happened in the story and how it ended had little meaning for him. Visual clues were not helpful because he could not interpret what was happening in the picture.

As mentioned, Charlie had excellent spelling ability. He took great pride in this talent and he could indeed spell many words. He often did well on spelling tests, which required the writing of individual words. His skills were so good that he could spell more words than he could read in context. But, as with his reading, when Charlie had to write the spelling words in sentences he struggled. Writing a sentence that expressed a complete thought was a mystery to him and he resisted writing if he could. He didn't get the central concept behind written communication.

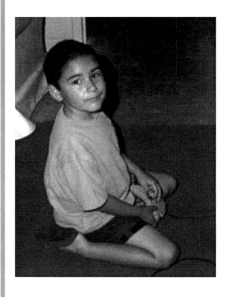

Charlie had excellent spelling skills. He took great pride in this talent and he could indeed spell many words.

Math was another subject Charlie enjoyed. He learned math facts to ten quickly, could rote count from any number to one hundred and could identify which numbers came before and after a number. If called upon to answer a fact problem Charlie was able to give the correct answer. He would smile with such satisfaction that he made his teachers and classmates smile with him.

Other professionals who were involved with Charlie's education included a speech and language therapist and the OT/PT staff. We were fortunate to have people in these disciplines who were eager to help whenever they were called upon for assistance.

Most of the families that had special needs children in our shared classroom were very supportive. Charlie's mother was no exception. Charlie was an only child of a single parent. His mother tried hard to reinforce some of his interests in and outside of school. She enrolled him in swimming lessons and he became a fairly skilled swimmer. In the summer Charlie attended a swim camp near her parent's home. When problems occurred or she was needed for reinforcement, Charlie's mother was available. She became an important member of the IEP team.

Maria

When Maria first arrived at the threshold of our room she turned to the EA and with apprehension asked; "Will it hurt her? Will it hurt her?", putting herself in the third person as she often did. She stood there frozen, peering into the classroom unwilling to enter. Debbie walked over and warmly greeted Maria. Taking her hand, Debbie led her into the classroom. As she spoke softly to Maria, Debbie showed her the desk with her name and demonstrated how to arrange the items from her schoolbag in it. Maria's facial expression began to relax. This five-minute introduction from her teacher was what Maria appeared to need in order to gain the courage to start her school day. Had this not been handled so sensitively, it's hard to say what kind of precedent may have been set for the year.

Maria's academic skills were not at grade level. She had a one-on-one EA who helped her learn and monitored her behavior. At times Maria needed to be redirected because she had a tendency to get "stuck." When this would happen, she'd shut down and refuse to complete an assignment that she didn't understand. When frustrated, Maria often tried to resolve the problem by striking out at peers and sometimes staff. For these and other reasons, her placement in the class was carefully considered.

Finally, we sat her at the back of the room so she could be removed quietly on those occasions when she lost control. That served to reduce her discomfort as well as that of the other students and the staff.

Unlike Charlie, at the beginning of the year Maria wasn't always able to reply to a direct question. She'd either repeat the question or make a totally unrelated statement that would draw giggles from some of the other students. Sometimes Maria would turn to her aide and wait for the aide to prompt the answer or have the aide give the correct information instead.

Like Charlie, Maria clearly desired to have friends, but was clueless as to how to gain the attention of her peers, much less what to do once she had. She was tall for her age and towered over many of her classmates. And she tended to strike out when they did something she did not like. Maria could be especially aggressive on the playground, where a higher level of physical interaction was within limits and generally allowable. These proclivities did little to endear her to potential friends.

Maria was extremely sound sensitive. She would cry uncontrollably when the fire alarm went off. Other sounds were so subtle it took us a while to realize that they were bothering her. For example, the echo in the girl's bathroom or the sound of people walking down the hallways seemed to be amplified for her. If students sharpened pencils or whispered while working on a group project, Maria was interrupted from her own work. She sat and stared until the source of the noise stopped.

Even when the room was quiet Maria had difficulty engaging in learning. She couldn't attend to a lesson for long periods. She seemed to have limited interests and didn't respond to many of the usual reinforcers in the large classroom. Maria quickly satiated on any verbal or tangible reinforcers used to help motivate her.

As stated, Maria's academic skills were not as well developed as Charlie's. Her reading vocabulary was limited and her lack of sight words interfered with her ability to read even the simplest stories. However, if she was asked to find something in an illustration from the story, she could easily identify it and point it out. While Debbie read orally to the class, Maria would sit in her designated spot and draw pictures from the story. Maria's art ability impressed the other students and as long as she had a picture cue to help her, she could get the gist of the stories being read . . . at least to some degree.

> Maria's placement in the class was carefully considered. Finally, we sat her at the back of the room so she could be removed quietly on those occasions when she lost control.

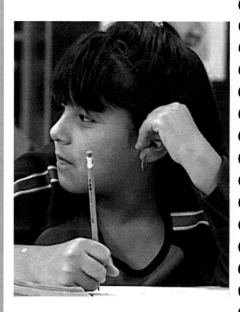

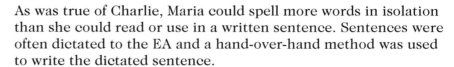

> It's often assumed that because their language is not well developed, students with autism can't understand concepts well. Jerry was a very bright child but verbally couldn't always express what he had learned.

As was true of Charlie, Maria could spell more words in isolation than she could read or use in a written sentence. Sentences were often dictated to the EA and a hand-over-hand method was used to write the dictated sentence.

Math concepts were difficult for her. With manipulatives, she could add to ten, but she didn't understand concepts of greater than and less than. Story problems were pretty much a mystery. Identifying coins didn't register, because the purpose of money wasn't clear to Maria.

On the other hand, social studies and science were of interest to her. Using visuals, Maria appeared to enjoy this time because she could work with the other students and tried to cooperate when prompted to do her part.

Maria's family was involved in her learning. Both of her parents assisted the school and tried to reinforce appropriate learning or behavior. Maria's mother volunteered in the class when her schedule permitted. Her younger sister could read and write at a much more sophisticated level than Maria. Despite being younger, Maria's sister would take on a caretaker's role when she interacted with Maria. Although she had good intentions, this behavior tended to further infantilize Maria. Maria, however, realized her younger sister was more skilled than she was. We all realized, parents and staff, that she needed to experience some success of her own and to find some activities that were her own. When the school year started, we were all still looking for something to involve Maria in which was totally hers.

Maria also received speech and language therapy as well as OT/PT services.

Jerry

Jerry was a tall slender student who like Maria had a one-on-one EA. Jerry's verbal ability was not as good as either of the other two students. However, he understood more language than he was able to express. When he did speak it was often with single words or short phrases. He tended to struggle more with academic concepts and when angered could be highly explosive.

His reading skills lagged well behind most of his grade level classmates. He could read a core list of high frequency words but often failed to demonstrate comprehension. Jerry had almost no concept of "story," and often echoed back the questions asked by the aide when she tried to get him to respond to that story. Even

when the book was heavily illustrated, he showed little interest in the story, nor did he watch videos or TV programs.

Jerry did learn a core set of spelling words and could write them when asked. But, like Maria and Charlie he had almost no concept of a sentence. Of all the academic tasks asked of Jerry, writing sentences was the one he resisted the most. His sentences were short and he copied them from a model supplied by the teacher or aide. Most of the time a hand-over-hand method was needed to complete the sentence.

Jerry did possess some knowledge of mathematical concepts and seemed to have some innate ability in this area. However, it was difficult to teach him new skills because he didn't seem to make the connection from one skill to the next. To him each concept was separate and what he had learned did not build onto a new math skill.

Jerry also had many sensory needs. He liked to be near his classmates, but he had little understanding of where his body space left off and a classmate's began. Some days he would wrap himself around a peer and other days he would strike out at them if they approached him. On occasion, and no one could predict what would instigate it, he would spring from his desk in full attack mode to strike another student, sometimes quite viciously. To say the unpredictability of his behavior tended to make most of the children leery of him would be a severe understatement.

Other sensory problems included a hypersensitivity to light, noises and textures of certain foods or other items.

On the playground Jerry tended to run from one piece of playground equipment to another. He needed constant supervision because of his aggression and his tendency to "dart" after the children lined up to come in from the recess. (In fact, darting in general was a problem with Jerry and meant he had to be watched carefully at all times.) Sometimes he would parallel play with a group of children but resisted any attempts on the part of other students to engage him in their games.

Jerry also had speech and language therapy, OT/PT sessions and adaptive physical education classes as part of his weekly schedule.

(Note: pgs. 59–61 are reproducibles. They include: parent questionnaire and a student questionnaire.)

> Jerry had many sensory needs. He liked to be near his classmates, but had little understanding of where his body space left off and another student's began. Some days he'd wrap himself around a peer and on others he'd strike out if they approached him.

> Darting was a problem with Jerry and meant he had to be watched carefully at all times.

Parent Questionnaire

Student's Name_____ Birthdate _____

1. What does your child do well?

2. What does your child like to do at home?

3. What do you think your child needs to work on?

4. What accomplishments do you want your child to achieve by the end of the year?

5. Do you have any concerns you would like to share (medical, behavioral, emotional, etc.).

6. Other comments.

Student Questionnaire

My name is _____

I like to be called _____

My phone number is_____

My birthday is on _____

My favorite color is _____

A great book I read this summer was _____

My favorite thing about school is _____

One special thing I want you to know about me is _____

_____

_____

If children with autism can experience a feeling of belonging in their first week of school, it can motivate their desire to become an accepted part of our class for the rest of the year.

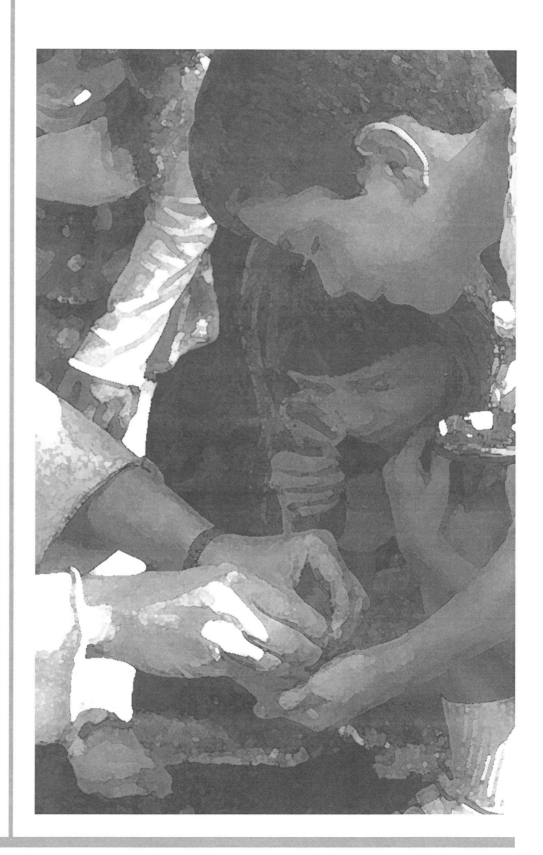

Chapter Three

Community Building

If children with autism can experience a feeling of belonging in their first week of school, it can serve to prime the child's motivation and desire to become an accepted part of our class for the rest of the year. For this reason, one of our first priorities at the beginning of the new year is to develop a sense of community within our classroom. To achieve this, we initiate a number of routines and activities that students are introduced to on the first day, some of which continue through the entire year.

Precisely because children with autism value their routines and strive for sameness, Judi spends a considerable amount of time in our classroom during the first few days helping them adjust to their new surroundings. This time was especially valuable for Maria and Jerry because their frustration threshold could be low.

Both children had one-on-one educational assistants, and this served to give their aides time to make visual schedules and other classroom materials that would be needed over the next few weeks. (It is important to note here that while we've been fortunate to have very competent aides for the children with autism, it's the special education teacher who is trained to teach and reinforce appropriate behaviors for children who have an educational handicapping condition. And it's important for the flow of the larger classroom that these children get as much time initially with their special education teacher as the schedule will allow.) Community building activities include:

'Favorite things' from home

On the first day of school, we give students a brown lunch bag and ask them to bring in three or four items from home that are special to them. We've found that having familiar items in the classroom tends to ease some of the anxiety students with autism often have when they find themselves in an unfamiliar environment. Anything can be included as long as it fits into the bag (hence its size) to keep pets or overstuffed teddy bears from taking up all our room. If you decide to take this approach, consider the following:

- Parents can assist their special needs child in making these selections. We encourage them to consider items that truly

On the first day of school, we give students a brown lunch bag and ask them to bring in three or four special items from home. We've found that having familiar things in the classroom eases some of the anxiety students with autism have when in an unfamiliar environment.

Anything can be included as long as it fits into the bag (hence its size), to keep pets or overstuffed teddy bears from taking up all our room.

BRIGHT IDEA!

We have a big bulletin board that's divided into 22 sections where students put up their favorite things from home. Charlie and Maria took pride in showing teachers or therapists who visited the classroom their items tacked onto the board.

Some of the children want to keep them on the board all year and that's fine with us.

BRIGHT IDEA!

represent their child. If parents are unable or unwilling to participate wholeheartedly, the special education staff can work with the child directly to come up with her favorite things. This is the advantage of having children on a caseload of the special education teacher for several years, because it gives you the opportunity to get well acquainted with their likes and dislikes.

✻ While all students participate and enjoy this activity, it may be most valuable to special education children because it provides teachers with some props to help ease new students into the classroom. It also helps familiarize us with the child's personality, especially the general education teacher. When possible, it helps if the parents place explanatory notes on the back of an item or in the bag.

✻ For children who struggle with language a "rehearsal" of how to share the bag is given to them outside of the grade level classroom.

✻ One item we really encourage students to bring in is a photo or hand-drawn picture that typifies a family activity that took place over the summer. If we know about an event and the child did not have a photo or a picture, then he has an opportunity to draw one at school. As stated, it's especially helpful if a family member jots notes on the back of the picture explaining its significance.

Once they have made their selections and have brought them in, all of the students have a chance to share their bag, including the picture, with classmates. In our opinion, it's doubly valuable to the children with autism or pervasive developmental delay, because it gives them the same chance to share interests as the other children and serves as a prompt for allowing them to do so. It communicates to the whole class that they have similar hobbies and tastes to the other children. We have a big bulletin board in our classroom that is divided into twenty-two sections where students put up their favorite things. Charlie and Maria took pride in showing teachers or therapists who visited the classroom their section with the items from home tacked onto the board. Some of the children want to keep the picture on the board all year and that is fine with us.

This activity is invaluable but also time-consuming. Sharing "favorite things" takes a good part of the first week. To allow for appropriate time to introduce academic subjects, and yet to give each child in the class a chance to participate in sharing, we have each student "show" one item at a time and work on the rest as the week goes on.

* When students are done sharing, a sentence strip is written about each child: e.g., "Charlie likes to swim." The next day the strips are passed out and each student receives one. The student then has to search for the child that the strip describes. This encourages the children with autism to associate and talk with other members of the class. The strips are put into a pocket chart for the first month or two and during free time the children can go and read the sentences. Charlie was especially fascinated by the sentences and knew within days which child belonged to each strip. Knowing something about each student seemed to give him confidence in interacting with them.

* Maria and Jerry were given a chance to rehearse how to present their bag and were prompted as to what question had to be asked when searching for the "owner" of the strip that was in their hand.

We also ask all students to bring in their favorite book or the title if they do not have the book. For children from families where reading isn't among the top priorities and who may not be able to bring ideas from home, we encourage them to recall a book from first grade, or show them the books in the room to choose from.

Classroom jobs

We understand that not all classrooms are set up like ours. However, most elementary classes have some part of the day that is driven by routine. We've found that the more involved you can get students in the daily running of the classroom the more investment they will have in the workings of that room. A good time to integrate children, who have some form of autism, is during the running of a daily routine. Because the routine is predictable, they adjust easily to it and often find it very pleasurable. And having them participate in classroom jobs also communicates to the other students that they are capable people and an active part of the class.

From the first week forward, students are introduced to a number of classroom jobs which are rotated through the school year, thus giving each student an equal turn at each one. Jobs include: Taking attendance and lunch count; calendar; daily tally of the number of school days; weather reports, and "teacher of the day."

The jobs assigned to students occur during the first half-hour of the school day. Since the children arrive at school from a more

A sentence strip is written about each child: e.g., "Charlie likes to swim." The next day the strips are passed out and each student receives one. The student then has to search for the child that the strip describes. This encourages children with autism to associate and talk with other members of the class.

Charlie was especially fascinated by the sentences and knew within days which child belonged to each strip. Knowing something about each student gave him confidence to interact with them.

BRIGHT IDEA!

BRIGHT IDEA!

If you use verbal cues in the regular classroom be careful of your volume. Some special education teachers were too loud and distracted the other students. That makes the special education students stand out from their peers, something you want to do as little as possible.

free-flowing home environment, not to mention time spent on the bus and playground, to the rather rigid atmosphere of a public school setting, the performance of daily jobs allow students to slip gradually into the class routine each day. In addition, every job has an academic component to it. Because this was a major transition for Charlie, Maria, and Jerry this was a time for Judi to be in the classroom to assist in a smoother daily transition.

The modifications made for each child allowed him to become more independent and to feel like he had mastered part of the school day. It also prevented caring classmates from jumping in and trying to "help" by doing the task for Charlie, Maria, and Jerry. By performing the same jobs as everyone else the other children recognized that these three students understood more of what was happening in the classroom than they were able to express verbally. Jerry and Maria had to perform the daily jobs without the educational assistant standing beside them. Debbie helped these two, as she did the other students. By insisting that the children follow her directions, Jerry and Maria learned how to comply with a request without being cued by the aide.

For every "job," modifications were made for Charlie, Maria, and Jerry. Not all modifications were successful. The ones, which led to academic and social growth, are listed below.

Lunch count

There are two choices offered in our hot lunch program. A third pertains to students who bring a cold lunch from home. A designated student records how many will take each of the options and making sure the sum equals the number of kids present in class for that day. Modifications include:

❋ Charlie and Maria could read and understand single words. To help them take lunch count the choices were highlighted and Maria was given a practice run at reading the menu before she took the count in front of the class. Counting the raised hands and having to write the correct number provided her with a real life experience in using math skills. In order to record the total, Maria used manipulatives at her desk to add all of the lunch choices.

❋ Jerry's aide went through the monthly menu and made laminated pictures of the lunch choices. When it was his turn to do lunch count he would look at the pictures and call out the choices from the picture cues. He also used manipulatives and a number line to add the total count for the day.

Calendar duty

There was a wall pocket chart of the calendar for all to see. Daily a student deposits the correct number for the date in the calendar pocket chart. The student also sets a clock to the time of day during which there is a "special" class, e.g., art, music, physical education, or computer lab. Below the clock the student writes the time in digital code. The student then reads the date and announces the special and what time it starts. For example, "today's date is Monday, September 24, 2001 and our special is art at 12:15." Modifications include:

❈ Each student had a calendar at her desk which was part of the math journal. When other class members gave the calendar date Charlie, Maria, and Jerry were asked to point to the day of the week on the calendar as well as the date. Therefore, by seeing a model and having a visual cue they began to understand how to read a calendar and by the end of the year the days of the week were integrated into their reading vocabulary.

❈ Daily practice of reading the calendar and filling in the dates was part of Judi's teaching routine in the resource room. The same verbal cues and language were used so that students not only learned how to read the calendar but could generalize this skill to another environment.

❈ Jerry and Maria were given three dates to pick from and asked what date was needed. They repeated the date as the teacher said it and eventually they were able to complete the task when the teacher prompted by saying, "today's date is?" and then pointing to the parts of the calendar as the student recited the date.

❈ Time and the concept of 'when something happened' tended to elude the three children. They were given a digital time to copy under the "clock" which was set for the special class for that day.

❈ Charlie was cued verbally where to look in the classroom as each job was being performed. When he was sitting at his desk, Judi quietly cued him and verbally foreshadowed the next task. At first he wouldn't look and had to be cued over and over before he understood the morning routine. If you are using verbal cues in the regular classroom be careful of your volume. Some of the the special education teachers

Jerry had difficulty remembering names of children in the room. Digital photos of each were taken. Using the photos, names were practiced in a one-on-one situation. When he was "class teacher," he had access to the photos for reference if he needed them. By the end of the year, he knew every child's name.

BRIGHT IDEA!

EXCELLENT PRODUCT ALERT!

Captain Tommy is published by Future Horizons, (800-489-2707).

have been criticized for being too loud and were distracting the other students. It also tends to make the special education students stand out from their peers, something you want to do as little as possible.

Class Teacher

Every month students are given a small journal to write a minimum of four math problems daily equaling the day's date. For example, on September, 24, a problem may read 19+5=24 or 30-6=24. All students are expected to write the problems either as they enter the classroom, or after assigned class jobs have been accomplished. They must be able to read the problem and defend the process that was used to find the answer. When the problems are completed in the journal, each student chooses one and writes it on the chalkboard. After all problems have been written on the board and the other class jobs have been completed, the "class teacher" comes to the front of the room and sits on a tall stool to call on every student. Each child reads the problem that she wrote on the board.

Each morning the previous day's teacher chooses the next one. Girls choose boys and boys choose girls. Debbie keeps a record so that everyone has a chance to be the teacher before the next rotation begins. Modifications include:

※ Jerry had difficulty remembering the names of the children in the room. Digital photos of each child were taken. Using the photos, the names of the children were practiced in a one-on-one situation. When he was "class teacher," he had access to the photos for reference if he needed them. By the end of the year, he knew every child's name.

※ Charlie and Maria were prompted by quietly whispering the names of the children. It did not take either long to learn and this modification was not significantly different than that given other students. Whenever these students had to give a group presentation every effort was made to make the modifications simple so they didn't draw excessive attention.

All of the jobs rotate through the members of the class. By assigning the jobs to students with autism or pervasive developmental delay it helped them feel a part of the class, and when they had a job the transition from home to school often was easier for them to make. Most importantly their classmates came to view Charlie, Maria and Jerry as students who could manage many different tasks.

Playground supervision

The first week of school Judi and one of the special education assistants take turns supervising the recesses. This helps the children learn the routine of hearing the bells, where to line up after the bells ring, and how to find the playground from either the classroom or the cafeteria. Judi also gives the staff information on how to reduce potential conflicts. A benefit from the additional supervision was that the more aggressive ED students tend to start the year without having discipline problems on the playground.

We Are All Alike

A final, but no less important, tradition early in the year is to offer an explanation of autism to the general education students: Maria and Jerry had visible behaviors which were significantly different from the other children in class. Their difficulty retrieving language made it hard for the other students to understand how to talk to them. When Maria and Jerry were out of the room, Debbie would attempt to explain, using a teacher-made book (see box at right), what made these students look and learn differently from the other children. One year, a mother of one of the students with autism came into the class and read **Captain Tommy**, a children's book written from the point of view of students with autism, and authored by a parent (Captain Tommy is published by Future Horizons, 800-489-2707). The mother answered the children's questions and sent a personal letter home to the other parents explaining something about her child. One amazing thing about elementary school children is how accepting they can be about people and how caring they are when you take the time to explain it to them. This is a major reason why teaching is rewarding.

Reproducibles:

The story Debbie reads to the class is titled **We Are All Alike**. Starting on pg. 70, there is a reproducible social story of this book.

We Are All Alike

We are all alike in many ways.
We have two eyes, two ears, a nose,
a mouth, hair, hands and feet.

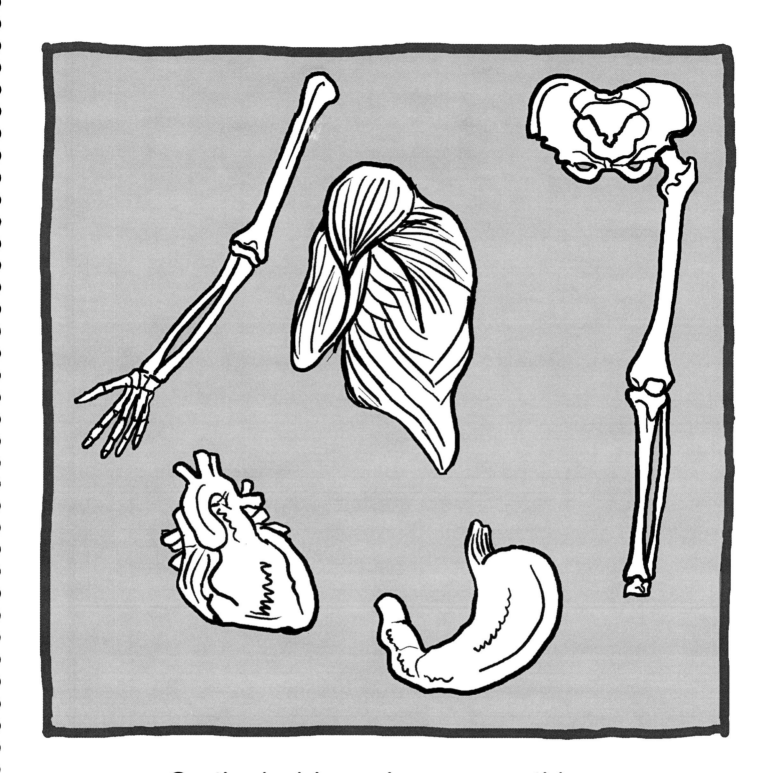

On the inside we have many things
that are alike. We all have bones,
muscles, a heart and a stomach.

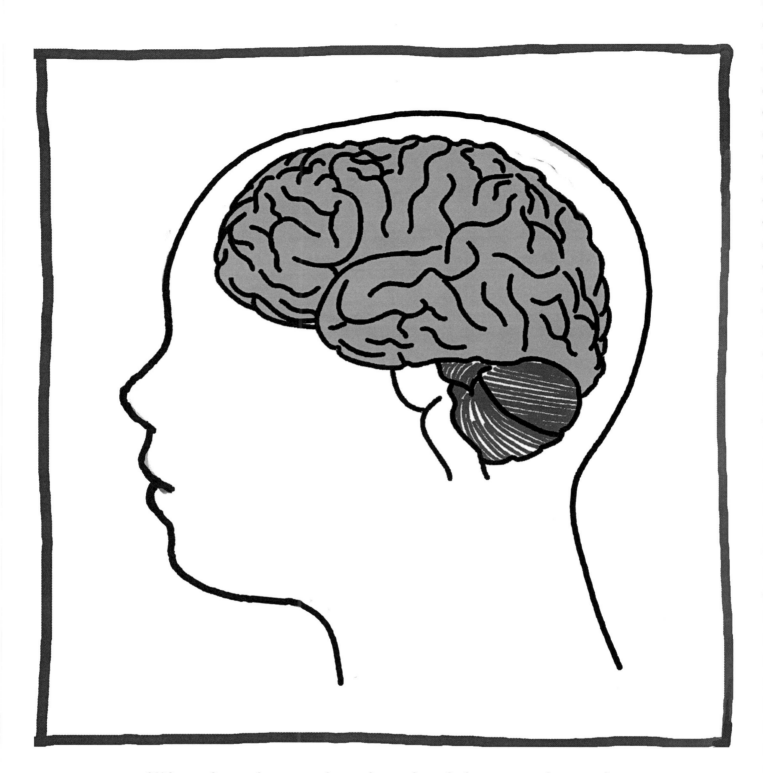

We also have brains inside our heads.
Our brain is like our body's computer.
Our brain is our message center.

We use our brain to solve problems.
Our brain helps us to walk and talk.

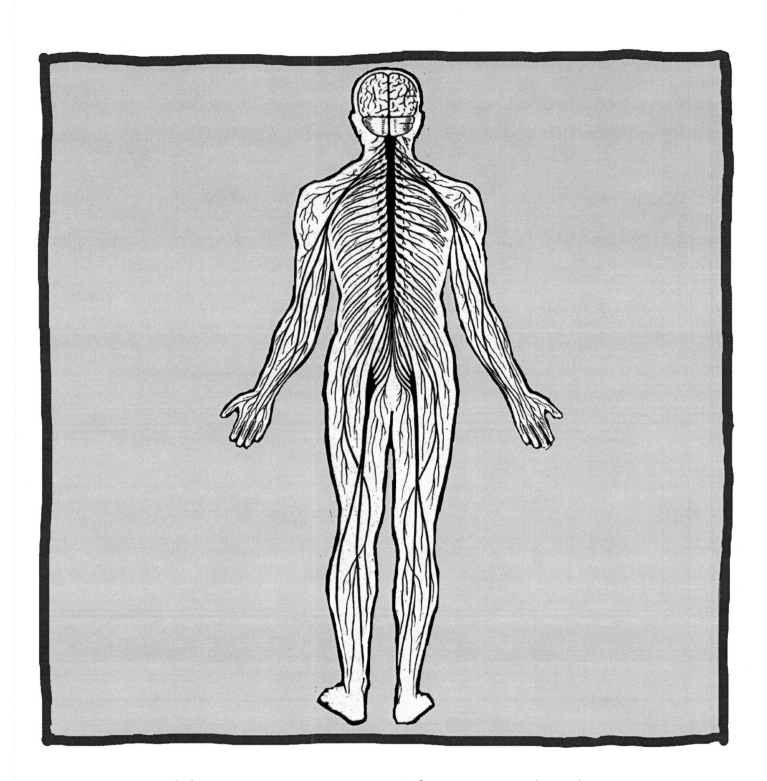

Messages are sent from our brain
to all parts of our body. The messages
follow paths throughout our body.

Children with autism have brains
like everyone else.

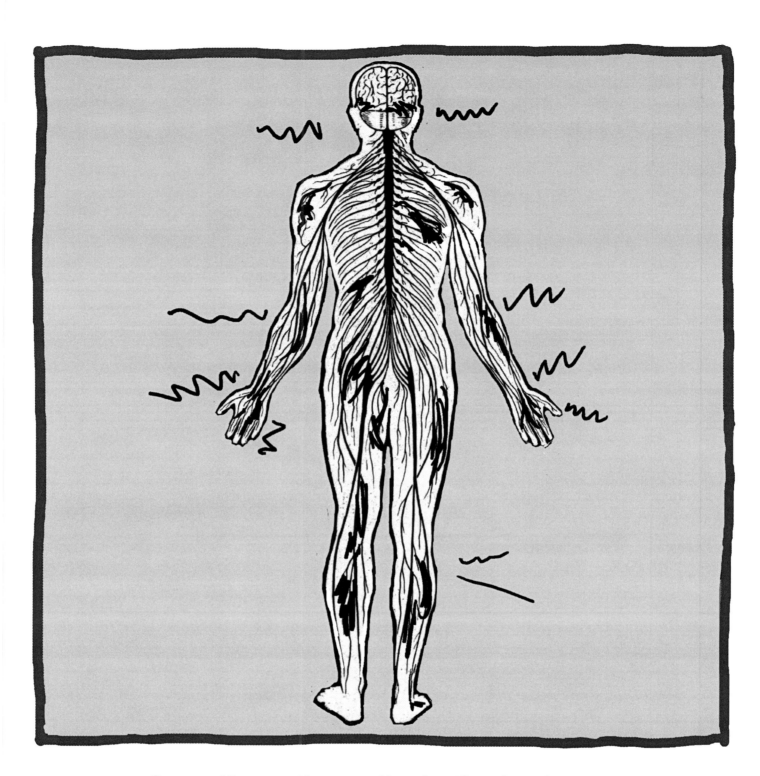

Sometimes the paths in the brains
of people with autism get confused.

Messages get lost as they try
to go to different parts of the body.

The person may know the answer
but can't say it. The message
doesn't make it out of his mouth.

The person may get frustrated.
The person may feel mad.

The person may do something wrong.
She may yell. She may hit herself
or someone next to her.

He is confused.
He doesn't mean to upset or hurt anyone around him.
Sometimes he can't say or do things like others.
That makes him frustrated and sad.

Loud sounds or unexpected noises
may cause confusion or pain.

Classroom lights, sunshine,
or newly fallen snow may be so bright
that he feels pain in his eyes and head.

Some food she eats feels funny in her mouth.
It doesn't taste good. She may only enjoy
a few foods that feel and taste good.

People with autism need our understanding.
They may say or do things differently than the rest
of us. But they like to do things like everyone else.

We can all be friends.

Chapter Four

Preparing the Resource Room

The previous sections of this manual have been centered on how to set-up a welcoming atmosphere in the regular education classroom for all students. Our goal has always been to integrate and teach students with autism and pervasive developmental delay together in an included environment as much as possible, although reality sometimes intruded, preventing us from running an all day program in the general classroom. At times the resource room is a necessity.

Interruptions could include: Academic and sensory needs which would interfere with total inclusion. Days when students were not physically up to par due to colds, headaches or other low grade illnesses that elementary students can be prone to. When kids with autism are under the weather, it seems their entire nervous system is thrown out of kilter. On those days when Charlie, Maria, and Jerry felt subpar, it was difficult for them to keep up the pace and they would often be better off in the special education resource room. In addition, all three had a chronic problem with sleeping through the night and on some days their energy level just wasn't there to keep up to the larger group.

Educators and parents need to be sensitive to the delicate neurological systems that students with autism have and not demand full integration everyday all day long no matter what their individual needs may be. IEPs need to be written with parent consent to allow for the best academic and social learning to take place because a major goal of any education system is to provide its students with the best skills possible.

The special education teacher can often modify the environment of the resource room to accommodate the learning styles of students in ways that aren't possible in the general classroom and by doing so provide a safe haven for children with autism to retire to when they're in a state of stimulus overload. The days before school starts are spent arranging the room so the environment is user friendly to all. Interestingly, it seems that other special education students who used the resource room appreciated the modifications to the physical environment as

> Special education teachers can modify the environment of the resource room in ways that aren't possible in the regular classroom and provide a safe haven for children with autism when they're in stimulus overload.

well. Often, they would ask for the typical light or sound adjustments to provide a more soothing environment, so they could concentrate. Many of the changes made in the resource room were due to consultation with a phenomenal OT/PT department, whose suggestions over the years have helped enormously.

Over-sensitivity to external stimuli

Sometimes students with autism seem to strike out or become agitated for no apparent reason. This sudden burst of energy could be because of a strong reaction to sound, light, or touch. In fact, even the texture of certain foods can be disturbing to them. Often playgrounds, assemblies, physical education classes, the cafeteria, and bathrooms are unfriendly places, even overwhelming at times. Be observant in analyzing the physical environment and change as much as possible to accommodate an overactive neurological system. This does not imply that students become aggressive only because of the structure of an environment but one needs to be sensitive about that before looking at other issues.

Establishing a user friendly environment somewhere in the school helps these children ask for accommodations which can calm them and in turn allow for more learning to take place.

Sound

As mentioned in the student descriptions, sound can interrupt concentration and distract learning. Some measures you can take include:

※ The entire resource room was carpeted and learning areas established so that some parts of the room were rendered quieter than others.

※ With Charlie and Maria we gave them verbal cues when it appeared they were having trouble concentrating. Simply ask if the place they are sitting is too noisy or if there are too many people walking past their seat. Constant cuing seemed to help them critically examine their own learning environment. Sometimes repetition of the problem and your insistence that they deal with it would help drive the point home. For example, at first Charlie and Maria tended to give predictable answers, which didn't always match what they were doing. If we felt strongly that we had identified the problem—e.g., they had been seated in a typically congested area—we just went ahead and asked them to move

---

> Other special education students who use the resource room also appreciate modifications to the physical environment.

Playgrounds, assemblies, physical education classes, the cafeteria, and bathrooms are overwhelming at times. Be observant in analyzing the physical environment and change it (as much as possible) to accommodate an overactive neurological system.

BRIGHT IDEA!

somewhere else. Then later we would provide the cue: "Maria you are working so well now! It helps for you to sit in a place where not so many people are moving by you as you work." Before the end of the year Charlie had begun to verbalize which sounds bothered him on his own without cuing. It took Maria another whole year before she could do the same. Jerry insisted on the same desk and remained dependent on the teaching staff to observe for him.

※ Since the resource room was next to the art room, noise coming from there was often disturbing to Charlie, Maria, and Jerry. To counteract that, we left a CD player on all day with environmental, new age, classical, or Gary Lamb's precisely synchronized piano music. All three students enjoyed music, especially Maria. She really took a shining to one of the Gary Lamb CDs (see box at right) and by the end of the year she would frequently ask to have her "favorite song" played when she felt stressed. Sometimes she would take the CD with her to OT/PT, or speech and language so she could concentrate during her sessions.

Our goal for modifying the room's environment was twofold: First, to encourage them to understand and communicate what their needs were, and to provide a suitable learning atmosphere for them in the meantime.

※ The use of headphones can help. When at the computer, Jerry often wore a headset to screen out classroom noise. He loved the computer and was quite gifted at it, so he didn't want be distracted from what he was doing. The headphones did not work as well for Maria or Charlie because they experienced them as tight and constrictive. But you don't know unless you try. Until all of these students learned to communicate their needs to some degree, we tried every approach we could think of and kept the ones that succeeded.

Overhead lighting

How many times have you been to a conference and heard you should turn off your fluorescent lights, that they are troublesome to students with autism and others? Probably more than once. But how many times have you been given alternative ideas for lighting a classroom? We learned a lot from Jerry, who was probably the most sound and light sensitive. We knew that once we'd lighted the room in a way that was acceptable to him, we'd solved the problem. We experimented with different

> It has been our experience that children with autism have responded well to soft, ambient music in the resource room.

EXCELLENT PRODUCT ALERT!

Gary Lamb's soothing CDs are available through www.garylamb.com

approaches before we found a combination of lighting techniques that worked.

First, we purchased a tall directional stand-up lamp that we angled to cast light on the ceiling rather than on the students. Next, we strung white Christmas lights around the whiteboards. Finally, night lights were plugged into all available outlets. In tandem, all of these different possibilities allowed for varying lighting schemes depending upon a child's sensitivity. When Jerry was unable to screen out the sound of the overhead lights, he was asked if he needed to have them turned off and then as each alternative light was turned on, he could answer whether or not it was the right amount for him to be able to concentrate again and resume his learning. Many of the other students seem to enjoy the more peaceful light and relief from the buzzing of the fluorescent lights. In fact, we've all remarked on how much quieter a classroom can be when all the fluorescent lights are off.

Lighting in general

Lighting in any situation, including natural, can pose problems for students with autism. In addition to overhead lights, other situations required other strategies.

※ Bright sunlight can be a problem. Since baseball caps are popular with our elementary students, we've had some luck in getting the children to wear them on the playground to help to screen out sunlight on bright days.

※ One student enjoyed sunglasses, again because other children and staff wore them. In particular, rose-colored or blue lenses blocked out the light but did not interfere with vision. We kept a small stash of glasses purchased from a dollar store and when students lost or broke them, they weren't a problem to replace.

※ Through consultation with the OT/PT staff and parents, we learned simple massage techniques to help reduce the stress on the eyes from light and to keep headaches to a minimal.

※ As much as possible, students with autism were seated facing away from a strong source of light such as the window.

A place of one's own

A quiet area for the student to relax in is very helpful, especially on occasions when the child is seriously stressed. For a while, Jerry used a large refrigerator box, which seemed to have a

Bright sunlight can be a problem. Since baseball caps are popular with our elementary students, encourage children to wear them on the playground to screen out excess sunlight.

BRIGHT IDEA!

calming effect on him. Maria preferred a corner with many beanbag chairs, while Charlie liked the motion of a rocking chair.

Touch

Parents are great resources for giving clues as to the kinds of tactile sensitivities their children have. For example, some clothing materials are naturally abrasive to them and a source of utmost discomfort. These are not behavioral issues, nor is the student acting out inappropriately because of these causes. Simply put, they are experienced as pain. Many of these students have had to have the clothing tags cut from their clothes. Charlie was ill at ease unless his socks were at the correct height and he could wear only one type of sock. Learning could not take place until his socks felt comfortable. We had to learn to be patient and wait until he had adjusted them.

* Thanks to input from OT/PT staff, we found that Maria and Jerry responded well to weighted vests, blankets, or lap pads in both rooms. Because they could cover the entire body, we generally didn't use the weighted blankets except when the children were agitated.

* Tactile sensitivities can be triggered by something so simple as sitting in a hard-backed chair. A "bumpy" cushion borrowed from OT/PT helped Jerry to be comfortable sitting at his desk, and since it was portable it could be moved from one room to another. Maria and Charlie preferred a padded seat, such as a swivel desk chair or the rocker, which was part of the room. These chairs gave relief from the hard plastic ones used in most classrooms.

* Again, consultation with OT/PT staff taught us how to massage tense shoulders and rub backs. Maria and Jerry usually responded to these techniques, and since we were discreet about it they could be used without drawing undue attention to the two students.

* To give children a visual cue as to appropriate body spaces, it helped to tape squares around their desks or to assign seating areas on the floor. Later, we also purchased carpet squares so they could be taken to special classes such as music.

* Each child had a "sensory survival box"(see pg. 99 for reproducible) in both rooms. These were small file card boxes filled with therapeutic tubing, putty, cush balls, large squeezable erasers, small cloth toys and sour or chewable

One student with autism enjoyed sunglasses, because other children and staff wore them. In particular, rose-colored or blue lenses blocked out light but didn't interfere with vision.

We keep a stash of glasses purchased from a dollar store and when students lose or break them, they're easy to replace.

BRIGHT IDEA!

Reproducible:

See pg. 99
for "Sensory Survival
Box" form.

Each child has a
"sensory survival box"
in both rooms. These
are file card boxes filled
with therapeutic tubing,
putty, cush balls, large
squeezable erasers,
small cloth toys and
sour or chewable candy.
It took some effort to get
them to use the items
appropriately. For
example, some students
couldn't handle the
temptation of candy
constantly at hand, so
we stored it elsewhere.
Eventually, they learned
to ask for it when
it was really needed.

BRIGHT IDEA!

candy. It took some teaching and prompting from the teachers and aides to get the children to use the items appropriately. For example, some students couldn't handle the temptation of candy constantly at hand and needed to have it stored elsewhere. Eventually they learned to ask for it when the candy was really needed.

⌘ We were fortunate to have a pool in our district. When the pressure of the school program began to wear on Jerry and Maria, an extra swim class time was available for them to attend. They were not skilled swimmers like Charlie, who swam competitively, but both enjoyed the water and after returning to the classroom were usually more willing to work.

⌘ We scheduled periodic breaks from the demands of mainstream instruction, which allowed the students to engage in an activity of their choice. For example, Jerry would select a computer program and totally immerse himself in it. Charlie loved to sink into taped stories, especially ones with background music. Maria would draw supple figures with large markers on butcher block paper. As the year progressed the children began to diversify their interests and would select a variety of other choices. Our goals were to find something that worked as an incentive and which became progressively more age appropriate: e.g., Jerry eventually stopped using basic computer programs and asked for more advanced ones after observing other students in his class using them.

⌘ Power walks were either scheduled or taken when the students seemed restless and struggled with concentration. We had light wrist and leg weights which we borrowed from the OT/PT department and we would find time for them to walk the hallways with them. Power walks became a popular way of reducing tension and renewing concentration for the other students on the special education caseload, especially those with attention and emotional disorders. A benefit of having students with autism is that they provide a model for you to teach others how to mange their bodies by using similar techniques.

⌘ We learned a series of exercises at a conference, which helped students with autism cross over the midline of the body. The exercises consisted of taking the right arm and touching a raised left knee, then a set of touching the back of a foot, then reversing sides. First, right hand to raised left knee; then left hand to raised right knee.

Repeat each ten times.

For some of them, starting the day doing these exercises seemed to be helpful. Maria, especially, would come to the resource room and perform the exercises before school. They were so successful, that eventually Debbie had her entire class do them before a major outcome or test. The LD students eventually also asked to start their learning doing the same exercises, since in the resource room they did not have to worry about peer reactions.

✻ One of the students was very thin and extremely sensitive to the cold. A washable throw was brought in and he put it over his shoulders to keep warm. The archaic heating system in our building was not always dependable.

Food sensitivities

This can be a hard one, especially if the children order hot lunches. Maria and Jerry could not drink milk because it tended to clog their esophagus and none of the students with autism could tolerate salad—it's far too rough and fibrous for their palette. The tricky part was in persuading the food staff that some of the "eating rules" needed to be broken and alternatives offered. We actually had a pretty discouraging butting of heads over this one. Maria couldn't drink milk but loved juice. The head of the food staff, however, was unable to see this as anything other than a play for special treatment. She insisted we get a "prescription" for juice for Maria. Fortunately, we had a nurse practitioner who was willing to talk to the food director and prescribed juice and other choices so that these children could drink something with their meal. When we did this, of course, the food director was furious. On the other hand, Maria was overjoyed. She told her aide that this was the first time she was able to have a drink with her lunch. It's important to note that the training of all staff in regards to the needs of children with autism or PDD should not stop with teachers, because they will also be interacting with food service, custodians and secretaries. These additional staff people can be strong allies or formidable enemies. Here, the administration needs to give you appropriate support, because some people are just not going to get it on their own. You, too, need to be a relentless, yet not pushy,

> Some clothing materials are abrasive to students with autism. This is not a behavioral issue, nor is the student acting out inappropriately. Simply put, they experienced it as pain.

> OT/PT staff can suggest alternative strategies which enable students with special needs to learn without detracting from the flow of the larger group. Make the most of your OT/PT staff.

advocate for the student.

❋ Drinking fountains seem to hold a fascination for all of the students on the caseload who are diagnosed with autism or PDD. Again, there are some battles that are not worth fighting. In order to keep Charlie from taking ten-minute drinks, he was warned that by the count of five he had to finish. By counting slowly it helped Charlie to gratify his thirst and gave him an audible cue to transition back into walking down the hallway. Allowing the children to have a water container in the classroom helped them from becoming thirsty in the first place and lessened their insistence on lengthy trips to the hallway fountain.

Scheduling OT/PT and speech and language

It hasn't always been the case, but our current OT/PT staff has become an invaluable resource for helping us grow as teachers. They are very busy and with the large population of children with autism enrolled in our district, their schedules are packed. They are especially good at suggesting alternative strategies to use in a classroom setting which enable students with special needs to learn without detracting from the flow of the larger group.

General education teachers are trained to deliver instruction and special education teachers are trained to develop modifications of that curriculum. But, in spite of the large numbers of children qualifying for OT/PT services, our teacher training programs continue to ignore even the most basic explanations for how to teach children to deal with bodies that are hard to control. The OT/PT staff tried to give the students with the greatest needs the first choice for scheduling. Make the most of this valuable resource:

❋ It's a given that most schools don't have as many therapists as they need. That leaves you to advocate for the best spots for your students to receive OT/PT. Considerations include: some of our students were not able to make the major transition from home to school and they were willing to schedule them first. Others started strong enough, but couldn't survive the long haul and they were scheduled for therapy towards the end of the day.

❋ While it wasn't always possible, the therapists tried hard not to take the children during important academic times. Some used playground and recess times to teach group and gross motor skills. Other therapists attended the physical education classes for the same reasons. Cooperation between this department and the teachers is vital.

- There were times when, upon our request, the therapist would come to the classroom and give suggestions on days when a student was really struggling. Looking back, we wonder how we were ever able to teach without their support.
- Our young and highly energized speech and language therapist also tried her best to help develop methods of communication that would lead to better learning. Her social stories were essential to teaching children appropriate ways to communicate and handle social as well as academic situations. She tried to meet some speech and language needs of our students in the inclusive setting. As the student's year is described in sequence throughout this book, the role of these specialists will be explained further.

(Note: pgs. 99–101 are reproducibles. They include: items for survival boxes and classroom equipment suggestions.)

EXCELLENT PRODUCT ALERT!

Carol Gray's "The New Social Story Book" is available from Future Horizon, 800-489-2707

Items for Survival Boxes

Things to squeeze

❑ A large green eraser

❑ "Cush ball"

❑ Therapeutic putty

❑ Clay in plastic bags (the non-sticky kind)

❑ Nerf balls

❑ Therapeutic tubing

Things to chew

Soft candy (preferably sour):

❑ Gummy worms

❑ Gummy bears

❑ midget Tootsie Rolls

❑ Mints

Food in plastic bags:

❑ Cereal

❑ Pretzels

❑ Popcorn

❑ Animal crackers

Other

❑ _____

❑ _____

❑ _____

Classroom Equipment

Items to Calm Restless Bodies

❑ Wrist and ankle weights (check with OT/PT staff for appropriated weight

❑ Weighted vests (consult with OT/PT)

❑ Weighted medicine balls

❑ Large therapeutic balls to sit on

❑ "Bumpy cushion" (another item which needs advise from OT/PT)

❑ Weighted blankets

Vision Adaptations

❑ Incandescent floor or table lamps (avoid lava lamps because they can be distractions)

❑ Indoor miniature holiday lights (preferably white, but it depends on each student what works best)

❑ Sunglasses or baseball caps for students who will tolerate them

Other

❑ Plastic water containers

❑ _____

❑ _____

Chapter Five

Rolling Into the Fall Semester

Just as the leaves start to turn, the class begins to hum with the fall routine. This is the time when we leave the previous grade review behind and the new curriculum kicks into drive. Careful planning is done so that all of the children can keep pace in their own way with what is being taught and have access to the general curriculum. Modifications are not only academic but also include classroom survival skills and social interactions that need to be learned in order to communicate with the many people who inhabit a large group setting. This is when careful observation by adults leads to a successful inclusive and coteaching classroom.

The first order of business is to provide students with a daily schedule. The schedule allows students to prepare for changes in the day and helps us foreshadow events for them. All the children in the classroom with neurological issues tend to respond best when a visual schedule is available. In addition, students with Asperger Syndrome, as well as other forms of autism, often find transitions difficult. It's important that transitions be foreshadowed and that each student has a visual schedule.

The first order of business is to provide students with a daily schedule. This allows students to prepare for changes in the day and helps us foreshadow events for them.

BRIGHT IDEA!

❋ Charlie used the regular classroom schedule posted on a small pocket chart. Time was spent teaching him where to find the daily schedule. This was part of our strategy to encourage him to observe the actual classroom for cues for what he was supposed to do. (It's these types of cues we take for granted that are so often missed by children with autism.) When the students needed to catch up on overdue assignments, Debbie wrote the ones that still needed to be completed on a special part of the board. Charlie was taught how to check the list to make sure he'd completed his assignments. He had his own basket on her desk where his assignments had to be placed.

❋ Routines are important for these children. Jerry especially tended to be chained to a predictable daily routine and when it was changed without warning he would often strike out.

Reproducible:

**See pgs. 117–119
for a sequenced
schedule form.**

Often people assume
that children with
autism are not
paying attention
because of the way
they habitually
withdraw. It's been
our experience
that, in fact, they
pay attention
to everything.

All of the students had a daily schedule presented to them as each day started.

※ Maria had a spiral notebook in which the day's schedule was written. On it, a large square was placed next to each scheduled activity for students to check off after it's completed. This helped Maria (and staff) from repeating again and again "When is art?" The EA or teacher could simply point to the activity and cue her. The schedule helped to eliminate some of her questioning and kept her from distracting the other students.

An example of what a sequenced schedule page would look like:

- ❏ Hang up coat and book bag
- ❏ Place homework book on top of desk
- ❏ Lunch count
- ❏ Two problems in the math journal
- ❏ Write a problem on the board
- ❏ Listen to the "teacher of the day"

It helped to warn her about any foreseen schedule changes and when a fire alarm or tornado drill was scheduled. Fortunately, the assistant principal was diligent about telling us so we could prepare our sound sensitive students. This was particularly true for Maria. Over the year, with practice on how to cover her ears and how to use self-talk, she became less afraid of the loud noise. On the way out of the building she would say; "It won't hurt you. It won't hurt you." Because she was forewarned, Maria could prepare for the shock to her hearing. It may not have helped to reduce the physical pain but she did become less afraid of the noise. This accomplishment made her proud, and after the drill was completed she would say, "It didn't hurt. It didn't hurt."

※ Jerry's schedule was made of pictures, which were laminated, and with the use of Velcro were changed daily. His schedule was as precise as Maria's, but it used illustrations instead. It was very important for us to review it with him and sometimes he needed it done repeatedly as the day advanced. Jerry would then remove each picture as he finished the task it stood for. He needed more breaks than Charlie or Maria so we scheduled "sensory breaks," which were inserted after he'd performed several short tasks. This allowed Jerry to work knowing he would soon have time to walk, get a drink or use the computer as a break from classroom learning. Both Jerry and Maria needed to have bathroom breaks included because they would forget to go unless reminded. We faded the illustrated schedule slowly, introduced a worded one and by the end of the year Jerry was able to use it without a problem.

✳ To help students remember where they had to go and keep on task once they were in the hallway on their way somewhere, we laminated an OT/PT card, a speech and language card, cards for special classes and a card for Mrs. Fischer and Mrs. Kinney. For Jerry and Maria (who had one-on-one EA's), the cards allowed aides to slowly back off from the students and shadow them in the hallways instead of having to walk next to them every step of the way. The card also helped Charlie, who often forgot where he was supposed to go, become more independent.

Reading

Learning to read and understand the reading material was the top academic priority for Charlie's, Maria's and Jerry's parents, as it is for most at this age. Accordingly, reading skills are probably the academic area most emphasized by elementary teachers. In their own ways Charlie, Maria, and Jerry expressed a desire to read better. Charlie told his mother that when it came to reading, his brain did not work like the other children's. Maria was aware of the fact that her younger sister could read better, because she read the books that Maria brought home from the library. Jerry would pick out a simple picture book and "read" the book out loud in an attempt to mimic what he heard and saw other children doing. Often people assume that children with autism are not paying attention to things because of the way they habitually withdraw, but it's been our experience that, in fact, they pay attention to everything. It's just that not all the stimuli going in is expressed in traditional ways you expect of children their age. Try to be careful observers of what students are attempting to do and don't always rely on language. Just as often their behavior can give clues.

Our district has a adopted whole language reading philosophy. Instead of reading out of a text, students spend several weeks studying an author. Authors selected represent a variety of books which have different reading levels. We start the year visiting the books of Eric Carle. (We are using Eric Carle as an example of the modifications developed for reading during the fall trimester.) He has a collage style of illustration that is often pleasing to young students. The brightly colored illustrations

EXCELLENT PRODUCT ALERT!

When phonics fail, consider **Reading Milestones**, by Pro-Ed, 800-847-3202.

To help students remember where they have to go when they're in the hallway, we laminated an OT/PT card, a speech and language card, cards for special classes, and a card for Mrs. Fischer and Mrs. Kinney.

BRIGHT IDEA!

fascinated Maria who tended to be attracted to colors.

✳ Using the information conveyed to us by Charlie's mother, attempts to cue him as to what he was expected to do in class were made by verbally prompting him to look at the other children and use their behavior as a model for him to follow. Of course, the children we used as models generally complied with teacher directions. Charlie, who was a quiet observer, began to use this survival skill on his own after much prompting. When other students got their books, so did he. If it was large group reading time Charlie was cued to look at the page that his seatmates had opened to and he tried to match it in his own book so that he was starting in the same place.

✳ Paper bookmarks didn't work well. Small sticker notes were easier to keep track of because they adhered to the book pages and could readily be removed. (Stickers often had pictures printed on them and Charlie's regular education seatmates began to ask if they could also use them. It was a small way in which Charlie could contribute to his reading pod.) Charlie had the coordination to use clip-on book-markers to help mark his place; he used these sometimes in place of stickies, so when the next reading time came he didn't have to flip through the pages as much to find where he was supposed to be reading.

Eric Carle books are heavily illustrated and Charlie needed to be taught how to "read" these pictures to assist him in understanding the story line. But, unlike Maria, when he looked at a picture he only saw the peripheral parts. He couldn't focus on objects in the middle. He could see the geometry of it but couldn't "read" meaning into the whole picture. We would take his hand and direct his attention to everything in the illustration. This was done by scanning over the entire picture using his hand and naming some of the objects. For example, "Charlie, let's find the hungry caterpillar in the picture," and we'd move his hand to the caterpillar. After many prompts, the hand-over-hand technique was slowly faded and he was verbally prompted to find something in the picture. (From **The Very Hungry Caterpillar**, Carle, 1987.)

✳ Early in his school career, Charlie was unable to color anything well. At the end of the Eric Carle unit the children used paints to do a figure in the style of Carle's illustrations. By that time, the illustrations had come to fascinate Charlie as he saw other children coloring their assignments using a

When Charlie looked at a picture he only saw the peripheral parts, and couldn't focus on objects in the middle. He could see the geometry of it but couldn't "read" meaning into the whole picture.

To help him, we'd take his hand and direct his attention to everything in the illustration. This was done by scanning over the entire picture using his hand and naming some of the objects.

BRIGHT IDEA!

multi-hued Carle-like style. Charlie began to do it too, and his classroom projects, including the required coloring, were as accomplished as most of the other students. Finally having mastered a difficult task brought that winning smile to his face, which Charlie used only when greatly pleased.

Charlie also had trouble connecting a series of written words. He could read some individual words up to a fifth grade level, well above his chronological age, but he didn't grasp that stringing words together communicated a greater idea. That was a difficult concept for him. So before a story was introduced to the large group, it was previewed with Charlie in the resource room. After the story was previewed Charlie read it again using the anticipatory questions which had been typed. At the top of each page a typed question was pasted. Charlie read the question and had to lightly underline with pencil or use highlighting tape on the part of the text that answered the question. For example, "What was the first thing the grouchy lady bug said to the sparrow?" Charlie had to find the sentence and highlight it. "Hey you," said the grouchy ladybug, "want to fight?" The physical process of having to look for the answer seemed to help him connect written words to their meaning. Using books written in a predictable style helped him begin to anticipate what would happen next. "What would the grouchy ladybug say to the next animal she met?" (From **The Grouchy Ladybug**, Carle, 1977.) Charlie was familiar with the story and when it was introduced in class he was better able to understand it. (Note: by the time Charlie was in third grade his reading skills were good enough that he was able to take the state third grade reading test.)

* In order for Charlie to follow directions on worksheets, it was read to him and then he had to highlight the directions on the second reading. This was another way to communicate to him that written words, taken together, conveyed a meaning. After all were highlighted, Charlie had to tell what he was supposed to do for that particular assignment.

* Repeated readings of stories gave Charlie (and Maria and Jerry) a feeling of familiarity with the content. The more each story was read the more they began to comprehend what reading was all about. For all three, repeated reading was a necessity.

* Both Maria and Jerry had small white boxes filled with short, easy-to-read books which covered similar stories being read by the other students. Books were ordered directly from publishers or the IMC staff helped to collect them for the students to use.

> Finally having mastered a difficult task brought that winning smile to his face, which Charlie only used when greatly pleased.

✖ Although she was often inappropriate in her relationships with peers, Maria enjoyed having the other children read to her. Of the three, she was the most people-oriented. In fact, Maria would rather talk to others than do her work. Either an adult or a student reading buddy would read one of the large group stories to her. Maria would draw something about the story. One day, after a parent volunteer read her the book, she drew a large beautiful caterpillar that looked just like the one in Carle's **The Very Hungry Caterpillar**. It was hard for her at times to access what she had learned because of her inability to verbalize personal experience. But often she could do it by drawing pictures. As she grew older Maria would state a fact, or blurt out something she had learned in the past but hadn't been able to express at the time it was taught. One thing we learned about Maria was that she was a deep well of knowledge who often took a long time to get to the bottom.

✖ Jerry and Maria received much of their reading instruction in the resource room. Jerry used a curriculum with a phonetic approach and Maria used a meaning-based reading series. Since both students had the potential to understand and access the general curriculum, the reading goal was to develop skills which would aid in achieving it. For example, they had to first point to a sentence which was read to them. Eventually they had to complete a sentence starter and use pictures to help sequence a story until both began to slowly understand that a story is more than a single event.

Spelling

We use a word chunking method as part of the spelling program. It's adopted from the Janiel Wagstaff book, **Phonics that Work: New Strategies for the Reading/Writing Classroom**. Chunks are identified (e.g., 'est' as in the word digest) from words found in the poetry lessons currently being studied by the class. After the word chunk has been identified, words with that chunk are brainstormed and recorded on a wall chart. Each child is then assigned homework to find at least one word from each chunk studied. They're asked to cut out words from newspapers, magazines, food labels, etc., and bring them to school. Their words are taped to a chart with the designated chunk. Hand written words are not acceptable.

EXCELLENT PRODUCT ALERT!

Phonics that Work: New Strategies for the Reading/Writing Classroom, published by Scholastic Professional Books.

- Charlie is a phonetic learner and he enjoys spelling. Therefore, he was eager to bring in words with the required chunks that had been assigned. These homework assignments helped him generalize the specific word chunk to a variety of other reading materials.
- Maria had a three-ring notebook in which her EA typed the spelling words she needed to learn for the chunks. For example: using the chunk 'an', Maria's words were man, pan, plan, etc. In her notebook the chunk was typed with a blank in front, e.g., _an. She was asked to pick a letter from a set of letters above the chunks to make the word she needed to spell. To help her to write the required spelling words, we used hand-over-hand prompting. With prompting, Maria would first write the correct letter then highlight the parts of all the words that had the chunk parts in them. This allowed her to begin to generalize that specific word chunk, since Maria had trouble grasping how the same word chunk could be found in different words. She then was asked to dictate a sentence using one of her words. We practiced the same dictated sentence drill everyday until she achieved mastery.
- Jerry's spelling list consisted of high frequency words from the first grade word list and those which he needed to write in his daily sentences: e.g., music, dog, gym, books.

Written language

Writing seemed a bit of a mystery to these students. Of all the subjects, written language was the hardest for them to grasp. Students who struggle to verbalize their thoughts in the first place also seem to find it difficult to put them down on paper. Charlie tended to do better on a keyboarding device, but Maria and Jerry were not yet ready to use the keyboard to express written language.

- It helped to have students stand in front of the whiteboard and look straight at a sentence. We found that putting large capital letters at the beginning of sentences was a good way to emphasize visually that a sentence started with a big (capital) letter. Larger than normal periods were put at the end of the sentence so students had a visual cue about where it ended.
- For Jerry to learn, sentences had to have high frequency words that he understood. Using a backward chaining method (see pg. 110) he slowly learned how to write a sentence independently.

One of Charlie's more poetic observations was that the crescent moon he had viewed the previous night, "looked like the end of a fingernail."

Backward Chaining

Usually, skills are taught by first introducing a concept such as writing sentences. You start the beginning of the sentence with a capital letter, write a complete thought, including a verb and end with a period. For children who may have divergent learning styles, teaching strategies need to be adapted, tweaked or somehow changed until you find something that works. As an alternative strategy for instructing written sentences for some of the students we experimented with a "backward chaining" method. We had some success with some students, and with them we continued to use it.

As with reading comprehension our task was to communicate to children that writing was an important skill for them to learn. (That written language communicated thoughts.)

To implement backward chaining, we used a sentence structure starting with the pronoun I, followed by a bank of verbs such as need, want, like and have. The sentences were written on a large whiteboard at the eye level of the child. They started with larger than normal capital letters and ended with larger than normal periods. The following is an example of how this procedure was used.

Step One
Try to elicit a sentence from the student. Sometimes verbal models are needed to prompt the student, such as: "I want a gummy bear." "I have music today." "I like the computer." "I need a drink."

Step Two
Write the dictated sentence on the board and have the student read it. Then ask the student to copy the sentence under the dictated sentence and reread the sentence that was just written. Next, the student is encouraged to write the sentence in a writing journal copying each word as the instructor points to it. This step is repeated until the student can give the daily sentence without having to verbally prompt ideas from the bank of words.

Step Three
Write the dictated sentence using the same procedure but eliminate the period. The student is then prompted to say what is needed at the end of the sentence and has to place the period in the correct spot. (Some students have to have a visual prompt such as a line or box to place the period in the correct spot.) The student again reads and copies the sentences on the whiteboard and in the student journal. Continue until student no longer needed prompts for a designated number of days in a row.

Step Four
Solicit from the student a sentence starter using the bank of words. Such as, "I want _____." The student then needs to write the last word and put the period in to complete the sentence. She rereads and rewrites the sentence on the board and in the journal. Repeat until the student can do this part independently.

Step Five
On the board, write, "I _____ _____." The student must complete the sentence independently and rereads and rewrites it using the above procedure.

Step Six
The student is able to generate her own sentence. (A similar method can be used for learning to write short paragraphs. Any kind of word bank can be developed. This was how we choose to do it.)

Mathematics

At the beginning of the year many math skills from the previous year were covered in review because all students needed the refresher. As we begin to introduce new concepts in the curriculum, it's important initially to walk students through them using tactile materials.

⁕ When Charlie first started to add teen numbers, we used Unifix Cubes of different colors to help him understand how to find the sum. For example, Charlie has eight yellow and five blue cubes, or 8+5=____? First Charlie had to state the problem, "eight plus five equals____?" Then he had to count out on his desk eight yellow cubes, followed by five blue cubes, link them together and count the total. Maria used a similar procedure.

⁕ Math was very difficult for Jerry. After exploring many different ways to teach him new math concepts we often had to use edible manipulatives. This was especially true of subtraction because he really struggled with this concept. He didn't understand it until we came up with an exercise where he was able to eat the amount that was subtracted. To keep him from having too much sugar in his system and to preserve his teeth, we used cereal or popcorn for the edible manipulatives.

Social Studies and Science

At the beginning of the year the science curriculum includes sections on growth stages of butterflies and moon observations. In the classroom we had a cage to house monarch butterfly caterpillars, and it was set up to allow students to see how a chrysalis was formed. Eventually we released the butterflies to migrate south. We used many picture cues and all three students with autism were encouraged to arrange them in order. One of Charlie's more poetic observations was noting that the crescent moon he had viewed the previous night looked like the end of a fingernail.

Social needs

The most important part of inclusion is to have the students feel they are an accepted and welcome part of the classroom and not just token members. As mentioned all three children really wanted to be accepted by their peers. Since Jerry especially would strike out, we counted on careful planning by all members

BRIGHT IDEA!

Math was very difficult for Jerry. He didn't understand it until we came up with an exercise where he was able to eat the amount that was being subtracted.

To keep him from putting too much sugar in his system and to preserve his teeth, we used cereal or popcorn for the edible manipulatives.

EXCELLENT PRODUCT ALERT!

Unifix Cubes to teach counting, from Teaching Resource Center, 800-833-8552.

When students had the opportunity to pick partners, we paid close attention to the ones who Charlie, Maria or Jerry selected.

BRIGHT IDEA!

of the IEP team to allow the other students to feel comfortable and safe in the group. For this reason, positioning of desks in the learning pods was important.

※ When students had the opportunity to pick partners we paid close attention to the ones who Charlie, Maria or Jerry selected. Charlie tended to pick girls or the boys who were eager to help.

※ Charlie and Maria had extreme difficulty sharing materials from their pencil boxes. To the other children that made them look selfish. Each had to be prompted to take a pencil or scissors and "lend it" to a pod mate. Both would stare at the child who was borrowing their materials until the item was returned. Charlie and Maria had to be taught that in order to cooperate with their classmates they had to share materials at times. Initially, they were physically prompted to give the asked-for-item to a classmate and at the same time we talked them through why the other child needed to have it. Charlie and Maria were read social stories on why one shares and we praised them to the skies for doing it "Maria, I know how hard it was to give the scissors to Jim. You are being a good friend by helping him out so that he can complete his work. Thank you." Reluctantly and slowly they learned and finally as the year progressed they didn't need to be prompted quite so much, though this remained a hard-learned lesson.

※ At the beginning of the year Maria tested the system to see if the "Rules" applied to her. When the students had to make a transition from one part of the room to another. Maria would stand up and hit a child then say, "Sorry." Or she would lean into another person or just stand and stare at the teachers refusing to move. To make these transitions smoothly, she had to be physically and verbally prompted. Also she had to be forewarned that a transition was about to happen so she could prepare herself for it. Maria was always praised and thanked for making an appropriate transition. She was not allowed to punch another child under any circumstances and often was asked to sit down again until she could stand up without pushing herself into anther child's body space.

※ Maria and Jerry insisted on being last in line. But this spot is a coveted position for all students and some of the other children habitually complained. The other students needed to be told that Maria and Jerry felt most comfortable in these positions for reasons that had to do with their disabilities.

We also told the other students that as the year went on all efforts would be made on our part to help Maria and Jerry feel comfortable in other positions. Maria was told that if the other children respected her need to be last in line she could not purposely bump them. As the year went along, however, they adjusted to different line positions. Both Maria and Jerry at the beginning of the year had to have an adult walk with them and prompt them verbally about the rules for walking in the hallways.

※ Maria tended to parrot back what was said to her or she would repeat the phrase over and over. Sometimes this would cause the other students to laugh or to mimic one of her parroted phrases back to her. We had to explain to them that one reason why Maria perseverated on certain phrases was because she needed to "talk out loud" in order to do her assignments. We modeled for them how to talk to Maria in an age appropriate voice and to try to ignore her (sometimes constant) inappropriate verbalizations when she was working. Since Maria tended to be loud, we worked on having her lower her voice until she could eventually talk in a whisper when, for example, she needed help on an assignment and other students were busy working. Once the class understood that Maria was struggling to learn how to talk age appropriately, they ceased to giggle so much and even at times tried to model sentences for her that were appropriate.

We had a similar problem with Jerry. He could speak in complete grade level sentences when he took the time, but he preferred to talk in short phrases. As a result students tended to talk baby talk to him thinking again that they were helping us as well as Jerry. We carefully modelled for them how to speak to him in short but appropriate sentences, and students tried hard to follow our directions. Most students will try to help you if they understand the reasons for it. As a result Maria and Jerry's spoken language improved and they benefited from student attempts to provide good language modelling.

It's important to note that we explained these considerations to the other students when Jerry and Maria were not present.

Riding the school bus

This can prove to be a major hurdle for children who have sensitive hearing and feel uncomfortable in crowded situations. Here again, social stories were important. At one point in the

> At the beginning of the year, Maria and Jerry had to have an adult walk along and verbally prompt them about the rules for walking in the hallways.

> Because of their naivete and lack of guile, children with autism are often easy prey for opportunistic peers.

Reproducible:

See pg. 120 for an illustrated social story about riding the bus.

year, some older children took to taunting Maria first thing in the morning and she tried to please them, in a sweet but sad way, by running up to kiss the buses as they came in. Needless to say, this was a very dangerous situation. We had to ask the administration to intervene and provide extra supervision along with a social story on how to come directly into the school from the bus.

A boy who was on Charlie's bus, who'd previously tried to steal his personal items, often teased Charlie and tried to con him out of his Pokemon cards. This could send Charlie right off the deep end and he sometimes responded by striking out, an act that only served to get Charlie in trouble. Again, we had to provide supervision as well as having parent support in regard to items that should and shouldn't be in his bag. Also, we did a social story on how to handle taunts.

Because of their naivete and overall lack of guile, children with autism are often easy prey for more aggressive peers.

Jerry rode a smaller bus with the frequent accompaniment of his EA. To prepare the EA, we walked her through the process of going with Jerry on the bus and did some problem-solving up front. In addition, we wrote a social story for him. It consisted of:

⚹ I need to wait for the bus with my hands at my side.

⚹ When the bus stops and the door opens I can walk into it.

⚹ I greet the driver by saying "Hi."

⚹ I go to my seat and put the seat belt on.

⚹ I can look at a book or chew some food while I wait in my seat until the ride to school is done.

⚹ I wait in my seat until the driver tells me I can get up.

⚹ Then I unbuckle my seat belt and stand until I can get off.

⚹ I wait for the children in front of me to get off before I walk down the steps.

⚹ I walk to the main door where my teacher is waiting.

Jerry's bus book had to be read to him many times during the school year as a preventative and his EA had to ride the bus periodically because he had a hard time staying in his seat and would occasionally lose it and hit the other children.

※ In order for Jerry to become more independent in walking to the bus we asked to have a line painted on the sidewalk, from the school to the bus stop, for him to follow and be able to get onto the assigned bus. The line gave him a visual cue to follow.

Bus issues are a constant for many students with autism.

Work habits and independent behavior

※ Charlie didn't have a one-on-one EA and he had to learn the skills necessary to complete work without that additional helper. When he was in the early childhood program he could get away with the occasional tantrum and striking out incident, but with his mother's support, and his desire to fit in, by the end of kindergarten his striking out was almost extinguished. After consultation with his mother, it was decided that Charlie wouldn't have a one-on-one aide for first grade. He seemed to be able to learn the rules with help from his teachers and other members of the IEP team, and he became more independent in his work habits by the beginning of the second grade. It was a tough call, deciding not to have an aide for him, but because he was able to handle it, it forced the responsibility back on him and seemed to be the best thing for him. You can always reverse a decision like this, but you don't know until you try. Sometimes you just have to take the jump.

※ Maria and Jerry need the extra assistance because of academic needs and because they tended to strike out. Our goal was to get them to a point where they could work and socialize without having to talk through a third party. At first, getting the EAs to back off a little was a delicate matter, because in both cases they were caring and competent, but we didn't want Maria and Jerry to remain dependent or to stick out any more than necessary. They also needed to learn to talk to other people and teachers and students needed to learn to talk to them directly. It's helpful to sit down as a team at the beginning of the school year and tell the EAs what your goals are for each student so they fully understand their individualized educational plans.

(Note: pgs. 117–129 are reproducibles. They include: schedule sample, schedule and Riding the Bus social story.)

Schedule Examples

Written Schedule

Day _____ Date _____

- ❑ Hang up coat
- ❑ Homework book on desk
- ❑ Math journal—2 problems
- ❑ Lunch count
- ❑ Write problem on board
- ❑ "Teacher of the day"
- ❑ Writing journal
- ❑ Break
- ❑ Spelling
- ❑ Recess   etc.

Visual Schedule

Hang up coat	Lunch count	Writing journal	
Homework book	Problem on board	Spelling	
Math journal	Teacher of the Day	Recess	etc.

Schedule Form

Written Schedule

Day _____ Date _____

❑ _____

❑ _____

❑ _____

❑ _____

❑ _____

❑ _____

❑ _____

❑ _____

❑ _____

❑ _____

Visual Schedule

Riding the Bus

I wait quietly for the bus to arrive.

When the bus stops the door opens. I get on.

I greet the driver by saying, "Hi."

I go to my seat and put the seat belt on.

I can look at a book or eat some food
while I wait in my seat until I get to school.

I wait in my seat until the driver
tells me I can get up.

Then I unbuckle my seat belt
and stand until I can get off.

I wait for the children in front of me
to get off before I walk down the steps.

I walk to the main door
where my teacher is waiting.

Chapter Six

Fall Conferences

After the leaves have fallen and students have begun lugging jackets, gloves and hats to school, fall conferences are scheduled. Parent conferences are important for all students. Since they're set up to communicate information between parents and teachers, they're especially beneficial for the education of children with autism. Usually, by this time, there's much to talk about. Besides information exchange, it's also a time for the IEP team to have input on IEP goals and objectives.

Most likely, you will be looking for a lot of important information on your students and your tack in seeking it from parents, who can justifiably be fragile and defensive, is critical. If your questions are worded wisely, it's likely parents will feel comfortable answering them. Part of this skill comes from sheer experience, the rest from careful preparation. And a great deal of groundwork on the part of both teachers goes into the fall conference. If all goes well, most will end with a renewal of trust for both the education staff and families.

Our conferences are held at night and students are invited. The format consists of a 40 minute block of time per student. Blocks are divided into two 20 minute segments. During one segment teachers meet with parents and students. The students show their self-assessment, the district report card is shared, IEP goals and objective updates are given and goals are set for the next trimester. During the other 20 minute period students share their major projects and school work with their families. Families are invited to spend as much time as needed to review the student's work from the beginning of the year. Many times one or more families will be looking at their child's work on display while another is meeting in a sectioned-off part of the room. Often, after the formal reporting of information, families will return to the displayed work again. Their child's best projects are always a source of pride and pleasure for families, as they should be. The student has a file of work that can be taken home but the big projects are kept for a memory book to be shared with the family the final week of school.

If your conference questions are worded wisely, parents will feel comfortable answering them. Part of this skill comes from experience, the rest from careful preparation.

BRIGHT IDEA!

Reproducibles:

See pgs. 139–145 for parent fall conference letters and forms.

Conferences provide a means for communicating progress and a time when parents can witness the interaction of their child with the teachers. Conversely, the teaching staff can observe interactions within the family, which can be instrumental for you in understanding the student's family dynamics. Some considerations when preparing for conferences include:

* Send home as much information as possible before the conference to optimize everyone's time and give parents a chance to think about questions they may have. (There never seems to be enough time to share and parents are encouraged to come in whenever they need to communicate their concern. Or they can call and set-up a phone conference.)

* All conferences are held in the general education classroom. All staff members who work with students enrolled in special education programs are invited to attend and to communicate with the family. Since conferences are held over a two-night period, students who have many staff members involved can have extra time if needed. Also, children with really large IEP teams can be scheduled before or after school on another day in order to give the families enough time to receive information.

* All the children's names and class times are written on the class fall conference schedule. This serves as a reaffirmation to everyone who attends conferences that the children with autism are part of the classroom community.

* Start by stressing accomplishments. Students (not to mention their parents) love to hear what they have done well and need to be encouraged to continue to make their best effort. Direct some of your questions to the student, since our conferences are child-led (see box on pg.133). Prior to the conference, we demonstrate ways for students to show and tell their families about their work on display. When appropriate, concerns about behavior, work habits, social and academic problems have already been communicated to the child. (And, throughout the trimester, to the families as well.) Every effort is made to prevent surprises during this critical interaction.

All the children's names and class times are written on the fall conference schedule. This serves as a reaffirmation to everyone who attends conferences that the children with autism are part of the classroom community.

BRIGHT IDEA!

Child-Led Conferences

A child-led conference is defined as one in which the student is invited and expected to come to the conference along with his family. Their value is two-fold: First, it gives each child a chance to show-off her room and her accomplishments to date, something students seem to love doing and that reinforces their connection to the school and staff; second, it's a great way to introduce their families to the school setting they spend their days in.

As much as possible the child is expected to lead his family through the conference: First by showing them the completed work in his portfolio; next any project he has on display on the exhibit table; and finally by attempting to answer questions posed by the family about the work displayed (some children need help from the special education staff). All of this must be accomplished before any discussion about student progress on the IEP or the report card takes place.

During the sharing of IEP goals and report card grades, the student answers questions and shows her parents the individual checklist she's completed, in which she evaluates herself as a learner. As much as possible praise is directed at the student. When a sensitive issue is addressed (one that isn't appropriate for the student to hear) arrangements are generally made beforehand for the student to visit one of the computer labs while the discussion takes place.

Child-led conferences allowed Charlie, Maria, and Jerry to feel like they are "can-do" kids rather than students who are continually left behind by the class's progress.

> Conferences provide a means for communicating progress and a time when parents can witness the interaction of their child with the teachers.

> Start by stressing accomplishments. Students (not to mention their parents) love to hear what they have done well and need to be encouraged to continue to make their best effort.

Preparing for Child-Led Conferences

※ Before the conference, students have an opportunity to rehearse what they say to their families and how to show their work on the display table.

※ Judi is with the families to assist the students, when needed, during the child-sharing part of the conference. However, the students are encouraged to talk directly with their families rather than through Judi. Jerry needed cue questions and when we gave them to him he was able to present his work. For example, on the monarch cycle diagram he was able to point to the different cycles when asked questions about each cycle. Like Charlie, when Jerry felt he had achieved something a wonderful grin would appear and take over his face. And after all of his work was presented, he would give his mother a big hug. When handled right, the conference process is a giant reaffirmation of heading in the right direction for student, parent and staff alike.

※ In order to be flexible to child and family needs, the format for a conference can be modified. In Maria's case the entire team came to share her conference. Instead of breaking up into two parts we met together for the whole period. As a team we helped Maria share her work. With some prompting she was able to tell her parents what she did well and point out a simple goal that she would like to accomplish by the end of the next trimester. Her goal was to be better at math. "Adding and subtracting bigger numbers, like the other kids." Her one-on-one aide had modified her self-assessment and Maria showed considerable insight into her own progress and behavior.

※ Charlie surprised everyone with his ability to complete the student self-assessment. Judi read through it with him beforehand, and he filled out the answers. His honesty and accuracy was amazing. Although many times, Charlie seemed to be lost in his own little world, it suddenly became obvious he was listening and looking. His assessment was very accurate and his goal for the next trimester was very appropriate.

※ Even with modifications, Jerry found the assessment to be difficult. But when given choices, he pointed to what, in his opinion, was his best subject and what he wanted to learn for the next trimester. Giving these children a chance to talk to their parents about school gave everyone important information.

- When we send the conference letter we also include an explanation to parents of our "two stars and a wish" initiative. (See box below.) At the end of the fall conference, we ask parents to put the two stars on the bulletin board and turn in the wish. Stars refer to two things parents learned at the conference that were positive indications of progress for their child, while the wish is taken into consideration when planning the next trimester's curriculum.

Two Stars and a Wish

Prior to conferences, we place a pile of sentence strips next to the portfolios of the students' work. Before their parents arrive, students rehearse what to say to their families to complete the strips. Each family is then encouraged to find two positive statements about their child's work during the preceding trimester and place them on the child's designated area of the student bulletin board. They often write statements like, "You learned many new spelling words. Your project on the butterflies was beautiful. You are a good worker. Your reading is getting better. I'm proud of you." If there's not enough time for parents to write them during the conference, we encourage them to take the strips home and have their child return the completed versions the next day. We find that written praise from parents boosts the child's self image.

In addition, families receive a "wish" form (there's a reproducible on pg. 141) on which they write a goal for their child to achieve over the next trimester. Their stated goals help us think about how to implement the child's program so their parents' wishes can be achieved. By giving parents input into their child's planning, it helps develop a stronger team bond between us.

Families of students with autism not only had academic concerns, these parents were concerned about their children's friendships and peer interactions in general.

Social Issues

The families of students with autism not only had academic concerns, these parents were concerned about their children's friendships and peer interactions in general. They realized that their children's social problems early in school careers would only worsen as they moved into middle and finally high school. So, we make an extra effort to keep them abreast of the progress we are making in these areas. Some steps we took to bolster students' social skills included:

※ We approached the OT/PT therapists and asked them to structure their program to include teaching children how to use playground equipment and how to interact with other students during recess and other free times. They also put together a computer skills scenario for us so students had an opportunity to engage in partnership learning in the computer lab. This was necessary to learn actual computer skills as well as providing an opportunity for interaction.

※ We gave Maria's parents forms for enrolling her in an excellent local fully-funded therapeutic riding school, an experience that was very helpful to her as it had been for many of Judi's students before Maria.

※ Although gym became too difficult for Jerry, and he was removed from his large group gym class, an IEP change was made to increase his time at the pool, an activity that was therapeutic and pleasurable for him. His adaptive PE class continued with support from the PT staff.

※ We generated a list of social stories, which included:
  • greeting people in the hallways and on the playground
  • how to take turns when playing a game
  • how to work quietly
  • how to ask for help

※ Instead of having the EA walk with Maria to the afterschool program (which was in the building), we collected a list of friends in her class who would walk with her. That allowed her to walk into the room with a friend like any other kid.

※ It was suggested that Maria learn how to eat appropriately when in the cafeteria. Up to this point, she would open her mouth when full of food to get attention from other students. We drew a short outline for a lunch program which included a social story, role playing practice for eating in public and selecting a small group of girls who enjoyed her company and were willing to eat lunch with her.

❋ Jerry's parents suggested that we set up a procedure for when he darted out of sight of his EA (since darting was common behavior for him). We drew up a short outline, which included a picture of him in the central office, assigning certain EAs to look for him in different parts of the school, and a special code (understood by all staff members) that was be announced over the PA system when he was missing. (*Note: by not using his name, we avoided further stigmatizing him.*)

❋ When Charlie verbalized that he liked two other students in his class, we responded by moving his desk to be near them.

❋ To reduce Jerry's frustration and tendency to strike out, we implemented more sensory breaks into his schedule. In addition, his desk was moved to a quieter part of the classroom, that had the additional advantage of being nearer to Debbie's desk.

When Charlie verbalized that he liked two other students in his class, we responded by moving his desk to be near them.

BRIGHT IDEA!

Exchange of information with parents or caregivers

We always try to end a conference with as much support for the families as we can provide. There are an infinite number of supports you can offer, depending on the child and the nature of your district. Things we have done include:

❋ Jerry's mother checked out a video of a classroom project in which Jerry had made a presentation.

❋ Maria's mother volunteered to help her read more at home and took a book home with her that Maria was interested in.

❋ Jerry's parents took information about a local parent support group that was being offered.

It's important that parents feel part of the educational process and can leave a meeting feeling like their child has made progress in some way.

The conferences provided an important opportunity for parents to see how the grade level curriculum was put in place and to review the expectations that all grade level students needed to meet. This was valuable information when setting goals for the next trimester. In general, Charlie's, Maria's and Jerry's parents seemed to appreciate our efforts to provide access to the general curriculum and to include them in classroom activities as much as possible.

Maria is now a teenager and we still remember her first fall conference. When it was completed, her father had tears in his eyes. He said he could not believe how much she had learned and how independent she had become. Neither of us has forgotten this moment. Sometimes educators in their anxiety and frustration in trying to teach students with autism and developmental delay forget how hard the families are working. After Maria's conference we've never forgotten.

(Note: pgs. 139–145 are reproducibles. They include: parent conference questionnaire, Two Stars and a Wish form, fall conference summary and student goals.)

Fall and Winter Conferences

Parent Questions

If you have any questions or concerns that you would like to address at the upcoming conference, please write them below and send them back to school with your child before the conference date. I want to be sure to allow enough time to both address your questions/concerns and share your child's report card. We will answer all questions/concerns that may arise during the conference.

Child's name _____

Parent's name _____

Questions

_____

_____

_____

_____

_____

_____

_____

_____

_____

Fall and Winter Conferences

Two Stars and A Wish

In the fall each child was asked to write two "stars" about themselves. They were to think of two things that they could do and were proud of. They were also asked to write a "wish," or a goal as to what they would like to strive to be better at during the next trimester of the year.

Your child will once again be asked to do this task. However, at this conference I am also asking parents to complete the same task. Please be prepared to write down two "star" facts about your child. These will be posted on their section of the bulletin board in the back of the room.

I am also asking you to write an academic goal for your child that can be reached by the end of the year. The goal will only be shared with your child. The paper that will be used will be provided at conference time.

Fall Conference Summary

Conferences are an exciting time for everyone. We have the chance to share work that has been completed, progress that had been made, and goals for the next trimester. It is important to remember that your child is expected to be a part of the conference. They will be sharing work that has been completed, and a self-assessment of themselves.

Please enter the room as soon as you arrive. If I am finishing with the previous conference, please ask your child to begin sharing work in the back of the room. Due to a very tight schedule, we will have to stay on the twenty minute scheduled time slot for each family. If additional time is required, I will gladly set up another conference time. Thank you for respecting the schedules of the other families involved.

At this fall conference we will be reviewing your child's social skills and work/study skills. We will discuss, if necessary, where improvement needs to be made, what progress is being made, and goals for the next trimester.

In the language arts area we have introduced the following:

- **Verbally shares information on a topic**
  We have practiced by telling the life cycle of the Monarch butterfly with the class as an audience.
- **Comprehends oral presentations**
  We have listened to a tape and written what was learned.
- **Applies reading strategies**
  We have reviewed and practiced the reading strategies that are to be used. Each student has had a running record completed by the teacher of a reading sample at the 2.0 reading level. Each student also has read with the classroom teacher. At this time reading strategies, fluency, and expression are observed.
- **Comprehends reading selections**
  We have written events of a story after reading selections and each child has been asked comprehension questions after reading orally with the teacher.
- **Expresses ideas clearly in writing**
  We have written a number of "Weekend News" stories where the main idea and supporting details have been practiced. We have also had the opportunity to write poems, and some children have begun writing stories about topics dear to them. We continue to practice proper punctuation, spelling, and penmanship.
- **Completes a graphic organizer**
  As we begin our study of rocks, we are gathering facts and completing a graphic organizer.

Student Goals

For teacher to record and track.

Time Period _____

Student Name	Student Goal	Goal Success

Chapter Seven

Winter Trimester

In our part of the country, the winter trimester arrives roughly around the time the weather takes a major and sustained nosedive. By now, classroom routines are familiar and students are comfortable with the expectations required of them during their school day. Charlie especially looked forward to doing a morning job. Participating in the same activities as other students, when he could, made him feel like a member of the class. His mother had been working hard on getting him to communicate some of this feeling of success at home and she was starting to make some progress.

At this point, we also revisit the goals their parents made during the fall conferences, which we discussed in the previous chapter, and try to find ways to implement them in the classroom. This chapter deals with the following curricula areas:

Reading

Our winter reading program continues with its "author studies" and adds a unit on different Native American cultures. More partner reading and large group activities are required of all students. Many of the modifications and adaptations started in the fall are continued. For example, we still provide Charlie with the opportunity to "front-load" stories in the resource room so he's ready for them when he gets to Debbie's room. We continue to ask questions about the illustrations and to cue him to specific elements in the pictures. As with the others, for his learning to be effective, Charlie required revisiting a story many times using different techniques to help with his comprehension. Some methods we found to be successful include:

※ **When reading him a story we divide it into ever smaller pieces**, asking Charlie to draw a picture of what happened at the end of each section to try to get him to understand that the words function to bring a "mental image or picture" in the reader's mind. As he was drawing he was asked to verbalize what he thought the section was about. At the end of the story he was told to retell it using his pictures. This activity helped him make the connection between individual words and comprehension of the story they told. Some days

> Participating in the same activities as other students, when he could, made Charlie feel like a member of the class.

We provide Charlie with the opportunity to "front-load" stories in the resource room so he's ready for them when he gets to Debbie's room.

BRIGHT IDEA!

At the end of the story Charlie was told to retell it using his pictures. This helped him make the connection between individual words and comprehension of the story.

Reproducible:

See pg. 163 for the six-square form.

Other students who had difficulty with reading materials quickly gravitated to Charlie's spot so they could get additional instruction. It helped reduce the notion that Charlie was the only one with problems reading.

he was able to do this type of lesson extremely well.

* During whole class instruction, a similar technique was implemented. Each student was given a clipboard and a "six-squared" paper. The story was read to the group in six sections. After each section students were asked to draw a picture or write a response in the respective square that answered a comprehension question asked by the teacher. Charlie would sit at the edge of the group with the other teacher next to him, quietly discussing what had been read and what his response would be. (See box at left.)

Not only was this option helpful for Charlie, it served a valuable secondary purpose for other students who had difficulty with the reading materials. They quickly learned to gravitate to this spot so that they also could also get additional instruction and it helped reduce the notion that Charlie was the only one with problems reading.

This quickly became canon: Whenever Charlie was asked to respond to a story he was always given the opportunity of drawing first, if he felt it would help him organize his thoughts. Often, this procedure was very successful.

* **For Maria's sake, we always tried our best to stay ahead in our planning.** This allowed us to locate materials related to our literature themes that were at an appropriate reading level for her. When possible we used books on tape that coincided with the classroom trade books we were studying. Or a staff member (usually her educational assistant) simply made tapes for her.

* **Pairing illustrations with reading materials** was also a successful tactic with Maria. But her affection for drawing created a problem we had to resolve. The students in her class were required to complete reading response sheets. They were then asked to write about characters, illustrations, author or events of an assigned story. An illustration relating to the story was also required. Because she so loved to draw, Maria took this is an opportunity to draw whatever came into her mind. This was fine to a point, but she had to learn that there was a purpose here beyond the joy of drawing for its own sake. We started by asking her to find an illustration she liked and to draw that one. She then was asked a question about the picture and using a hand over hand technique we wrote together her response at the bottom of the page. Slowly Maria began to understand that there were times for "fun" art and others times she

needed to do "work" art.

Maria continued to enjoy story time and would draw events from the story on her board. It helped considerably with her comprehension of the individual student reading assignments.

※ **Jerry, at this point in the school year, was taking most of his reading instruction when he was out of the general classroom**, though twice a week he was still involved with class independent reading time. He had a special seat near the teacher's desk where he was given a container of books from which to pick. Using an eraser at the end of a pencil to follow along with the text, Jerry would softly read his book. On these days, Debbie put him on the list of children to listen to read. This gave her an opportunity to hear how much he was learning and Jerry seemed to be pleased that he was part of a reading pod. Even though he was not decoding every word, he was verbalizing the story and he became more interested in the illustrations than he had been at the beginning of the year. He liked sitting next to the teacher and it was an opportunity for him to be included without his aide "hovering" over him. Jerry would look up from his reading at the other students from time to time and smile. Because of his fierce insistence on having his own body space, on days when he seemed to be struggling with this issue he was asked if he wanted to read near the teacher. If he said no, Debbie would tell him that she would listen to him read from the space in which he felt most comfortable. Some days it was difficult for Jerry to read out loud. Instead, he was given the opportunity to read the book by himself in the chair that was near Debbie. Jerry still had to read but he was given an opportunity to do the assignment in a different way.

※ Every day the class was given a time to read independently (B.E.A.R. Time: **B**eary **E**xcited **A**bout **R**eading). During this time Debbie would read with five different children each day, while Judi taught additional reading skills to Charlie, Maria and Jerry (on days when they weren't scheduled to read with Debbie). This was a time for us to emphasize the reading strategies we were teaching to the students. At the end of the reading of a passage or short story they were asked to retell a small part of the text or were given yes/no questions as in Jerry's case.

Jerry was pleased to be part of the reading pod.

Jerry liked sitting next to the teacher. It gave him a chance to be included without his aide "hovering" over him.

Build in a success factor any way you can. For example, during group discussions Charlie's and Maria's hands were usually raised to answer questions. We called on them when we knew they had already rehearsed how to answer the questions.

BRIGHT IDEA!

✳ Build in a success factor any way you can. For example, during group discussions Charlie's and Maria's hands were usually raised to answer questions. We called on them when we knew they were sure of the answer because they had already rehearsed how to answer certain questions. This proved especially beneficial, because eventually their classmates began to perceive them as having some strong skills. After Jerry started to understand parts of a story, we asked him questions which were always worded in the same way so he could contribute to the class discussions when appropriate. Often the other students would voluntarily praise him for his answer and he would quietly grin. Jerry responded well to group praise.

Creative Writing

Creative writing assignments continued to be more difficult for all three students. This is to be expected because writing in general tends to be difficult for elementary school students. Monday mornings always start with a creative writing assignment concerning events that happened over the weekend. The students are asked to write about their experiences and to draw a picture, which represented something they had written about.

✳ For Charlie, we made sentence strips from details he told us about his weekend. We needed to prompt him with questions and on some mornings when it was difficult for him to remember, we had him draw a picture of what he had done and this visual aid would usually stir his memory. Then, starting from the picture we asked questions to help generate sentences. The sentences were then numbered and put in order based on Charlie's information. He would copy these sentences into his weekend journal to read and share with the rest of the class. Teacher reinforcement was given throughout the entire task. We constantly strove to connect his pictures or "mental images" to his writing as well as to his reading. Slowly, Charlie began to make the connection though some days it was a challenge for him.

✳ Since Maria already had visual acuity, we knew we could draw on her artistic interest as a supplementary aid to her writing. Usually with her, we would start with drawing and work our way into writing. Her parents contributed greatly by writing notes to us in her homework book about anything special she'd done over the weekend to help generate ideas for the Monday morning activity. Again we prepared sentence strips and started each sentence with a word to help her sequence her ideas. Such as, "The first thing I did. The second thing I did. . . The last thing I did was. . ." We also numbered the strips to help her grasp the concept of how writing follows a logical sequence. At first, Maria needed the help of hand-over-hand assistance. But at the first opportunity, we began to fade it by telling her we would help her do all the sentences but the last one, which she had to do on her own. Then we slowly increased the amount of sentences and words that she had to copy by herself. Eventually we got to the point where we asked her how much she thought she could do by herself and really praised her efforts at becoming more independent in her writing. Between the fading, the praise and the growing sense of accomplishment, she edged ever forward towards independence.

※ Jerry, by this time, had progressed to being able to write a complete sentence on his own on the large whiteboard in the room. When he was asked, one of us would write "I" on the board and Jerry would finish the sentence. Then, he'd copy it into his writing journal as the teacher pointed to each word. He was encouraged to draw his own illustrations but sometimes he needed the picture outlined. We always made it a point to ask whether or not he needed this done for him, because he also was striving to become more independent in his work. Jerry always shared his weekend journal with the other students.

※ It was not always possible to use keyboarding devices (e.g., computers or Alpha-Smart) for writing, but whenever they were available, both Charlie and Jerry used them. Maria, on the other hand, was much more people-oriented and it wasn't until she was older that she learned to appreciate keyboarding devices. The computer fascinated the other two students, however, and Charlie especially enjoyed checking his spelling against the spell checker. Jerry carefully observed other children using computers and he mimicked their behavior as much as he could.

(Note: This is one reason why carefully guided inclusion is so effective: because children learn so much from modeling after other children.)

> We made sentence strips for Charlie from details he told us about his weekend. We prompted him with questions and on mornings when he was struggling, we had him draw a picture of what he had done. This visual aid usually stirred his memory.

> Since Maria had visual acuity, we knew we could draw on her artistic interest as an aid to her writing.

> For Charlie, basic math concepts are a strength. It was only when he was asked to solve story problems that he'd run into trouble.

Math

By this point in the year, the math curriculum has typically begun to encompass more complicated concepts. With greater and greater frequency, students are introduced to story problems which they are asked to solve. Daily math skills such as telling time, counting money, and measuring are taught.

※ For Charlie, basic math concepts are a strength. It was only when he was asked to solve story problems that he'd run into trouble. There, extra instruction was required. So at the same time that we were working on an area that he struggled with, we also decided we needed to work on helping Charlie learn how to ask for assistance when he needed it. He had to be constantly encouraged to participate, at least at first. For example, we had to actively urge him to raise his hand instead of sitting in his seat staring at the page or putting the assignment in his desk because he didn't understand it. He was also given the option of completing the work in the general classroom with teacher help, or go to a quieter and more self-contained room. Charlie became more adept at figuring out what kind of instruction he needed for that day's math assignments and at communicating his needs to us.

※ Maria and Jerry remained in the classroom for the daily math problems. They continued to use manipulatives and write the daily math problem in their math journals. Some days it was necessary to dot out the problem and encourage the students to trace it. Taking the math journal with them, Jerry and Maria would write the problem on their own on the board to recite to the larger group.

※ When Maria had to work math problems in a smaller classroom, she used a Talking Calculator (see box at left), which she found very helpful.

※ Story problems were modified for Maria by using numbers to twenty and she had her own notebook in which the staff wrote story problems based on her interests. Eventually, addition problems were written with a blank for Maria to add her own numbers. Maria again traced number sentences and labels as she orally repeated the problem.

※ Jerry's story problems were limited to two each day and were written for the purpose of using manipulatives available in the room. For example, "Jerry had five red teddy bears (he was given five small red bears) and Sara gave him three yellow bears (he was given three additional bears). How many does Jerry have now?" Jerry had to count the bears and put the correct number in the number sentence; e.g., 5 bears + 3 bears = 8 bears. He then had to count all of the bears and was asked how many he had altogether. Eventually Jerry was able to come up with his own numbers when presented with a number sentence.

✳ Jerry's strong interest in, and abilities with the computer allowed us to teach more sophisticated math skills and to reinforce those he already knew. Because of the way the programs were written it was easier for him to understand when he was successful and he could spend longer at a computer program than he could using pencil and paper. However, he didn't spend his entire math lesson at the computer, but performed a mixture of both instructional methods.

Social Studies and Science

Charlie and Maria had an interest in science and enjoyed the science kit work, especially when activities required manipulatives, which really seemed to help them understand what was being taught. We continued foreshadowing with both of them in the resource room to prepare them for the inclusion environment and Maria surprised everyone during the solids and liquids unit by being able to tell the differences between them and ordering solids based on their weight and size.

A problem that arose, however, was that the other students in her group would talk to Maria's EA if she was there to help. One of our goals, of course, was to encourage direct communication between Maria and the other students without the benefit of an intermediary. Finally, we had to intervene and make it clear to them that they needed to address their comments to Maria instead. This took some monitoring before the children felt comfortable doing this, but eventually it was successful.

Charlie received some extra assistance from one of the teachers in how to interact in his science group, which was helpful to him and allowed him to participate more fully in the classroom activities. It's worth mentioning again (and again and again) that a little extra work in interactive and social skill areas with students with autism equals academic instruction, because while they struggle with it so much, the more they improve their skills in these areas, the more their academic skills are enhanced. And when you add to this mix the fact that so many students with autism have tremendous potential and are very bright, there is

> Story problems were modified for Maria by using numbers to twenty and she had her own notebook in which the staff wrote story problems based on her interests.

The other students would often talk to her EA instead of Maria.

We stressed direct communication between Maria and the others, without the benefit of an intermediary.

BRIGHT IDEA!

Many students with autism are very bright, so there is significant motivation to improve social and communication skills and take advantage of their academic potential.

significant motivation to improve both social and communication skills to free up their academic abilities for full expression.

We had a little more difficulty educating Jerry in the academic areas, because his parents continued to have a different set of priorities about what and how he should learn. In short, they insisted that he remain in the general social studies/science class. This impulse, while admirable, left us in a position where we were unable to foreshadow and prepare him for success in the open classroom. It's a dilemma we expect many of you are facing out there today with the increased emphasis on parent advocacy and parent rights. It's certainly not that we reject parental involvement. On the contrary, we have spent most of our years as teachers encouraging it. However, there are times when we wish these parents would trust our judgement on issues like resource room preps that are helpful for their children, rather than worrying about the ideal of "total inclusion all of the time."

To get back off the soapbox, as with all teachers, we play the hand we are given. We spent considerable time looking at the major concepts of these curriculum areas and attempting to find those parts which would enhance Jerry's background knowledge as well as information that he needed to know to be more successful in science and social studies for the following year. We used a lot of computer-generated clip art for the social studies curriculum. His EA spent her prep time making special booklets with the clip art in it so that he could get the main idea of each unit.

In science, it helped to give him some of the materials from the kits, and we found that by using tactile and hands-on approaches when we could, he was able to match words to a concept. For example, he had to discriminate between a liquid and a solid. He had to place the word liquid next to the liquid and the word solid next to the solid. He learned that liquids are wet because he could pour it over his hand and that solids were not wet because he could not pour them. Our school takes an outcome-based approach, so the outcome assessments were modified in these areas to test only those skill that Jerry learned.

Friendships and Play:

❋ Social skills, social skills, social skills. . . one of Charlie's mother's major stated goals at the fall conference was her desire to have him feel more comfortable with friendships. His lack of affect and guile, and his general uneasiness in social interactions continued to hamper his ability to relate to his age mates. And, as so often is the case, when communication skills are subpar, it impacts negatively on the ability to function in other areas, notably academic. Therefore, this had always been a priority for us as well as for his mother.

❋ When working with a partner on classroom activities, Charlie was given the chance to choose whom he was to be paired with for that lesson. We could then see which classmates he felt comfortable working with and we could go one step further and apply his choices to other activities, thus helping him develop friendships. Here's where parental collaboration really helps. Charlie was enrolled in the winter soccer league and he continued his swimming lessons as a way to interact with others and to develop confidence. Charlie was a pretty good swimmer and it gave him a chance to show off his abilities.

❋ The PT staff assisted Charlie on the playground to strengthen those interactive skills necessary to participate successfully in some activities. Part of the session in the therapy room involved ball-handling skills, so that with their guidance Charlie was able to practice skills he needed to use for the indoor soccer league.

❋ The speech and language teacher pitched in by working closely with us on social stories. She would develop a script for us involving whatever skill we were working on, and then Judi and her EA took photos of the children enacting the appropriate skill areas. (Judi took several photography classes from a local night school to improve her skills in this area.) A student in another classroom, who was also on Judi's caseload, was an aspiring actress, and she helped Charlie, Maria and Jerry with the pictures. We would tell her what each picture was supposed to be about and because she was so naturally dramatic in her presentation of the skill, Charlie would laugh when he saw the picture and could easily identify what the picture was about. The photos and script were put into a social story, which then was read to the target student everyday for two weeks. In addition, we

The PT staff assisted Charlie on the playground to strengthen interactive skills necessary to participate successfully in some activities.

BRIGHT IDEA!

> Maria's mother was willing to reinforce appropriate school behavior and help us work with aggressive behaviors in any way possible.

> Her striking out incidences decreased considerably, because the home/school communication helped give Maria consistent guidelines for her behavior.

made extra copies to send home for the families to read on the weekends.

※ During the fall conference, Maria's parents expressed concern about her continued aggression and asked for a plan to help teach her more appropriate behaviors as well as to extinguish the more contentious ones. At that time, Maria's mother stated she was willing to reinforce appropriate school behavior and help us work with the aggressive behaviors in whatever way possible. Since Maria was very attached to her family, we knew she would try hard to adhere to family rules when she was able to do it.

We worked out a plan to have Maria's mother reinforce her daily behavior based on our feedback. She was asked to reinforce Maria when she was able to get through a day without being aggressive and by following the class rules. If an incident occurred Maria had to immediately call her mother at work and explain what had happened at school. (This requires a lot of commitment on any parent's part and for some simply isn't possible. After all, we don't all have understanding employers.)

When called, Maria's mother would tell her the consequences for striking out or other noncompliant behavior. It took time, but it was very effective. Maria learned that when frustrated she had to find a less aggressive way of handling a situation. Her striking out incidences decreased considerably and the home/school communication helped give her consistent guidelines for her behavior. The school staff appreciated the support and Maria was happier because more classmates were willing to be with her on the playground.

※ In addition, our school psychologist, who always took a keen interest in developing special programming for our students with autism, met with Maria and helped to establish a Circle of Friends group with several girls who volunteered to join her for lunch break on a regular basis. These contacts carried over to the classroom and further helped bolster Maria's standing with classmates.

※ Maria's family enrolled her in a wonderful, local therapeutic riding school. Maria enjoyed the lessons because they were something she could do that was her own hobby/activity. Many of the students appreciated the photos she brought in of "her horse" and riding teacher.

※ By the time the days began to darken and the snow filters quickly through momentarily opened doors, Jerry was finding it too difficult to come directly from the bus to the second grade classroom. The crowding around the coat area provided a stimulus overload and was too much for him to manage. He quickly became irritated by the jostling of coats and bodies and that wasn't a state we wanted him to be in.

So we adjusted his schedule to allow him to hang his coat outside of the resource room and to come directly into the classroom first thing in the morning. Since there already were students in the room, he was greeted in a friendly but subdued manner and it allowed him to acclimate to his surroundings. After he had a chance to preview his day's schedule without commotion, Jerry was able to walk to the regular classroom after the halls were cleared, to start his morning routine.

※ We found two older boys who were willing to mentor and help Jerry and he responded to them immediately. The PE teacher recruited one of them to help in the Adaptive Physical Education Class, providing Jerry with his own student tutor to teach him to throw balls and to use some of the equipment to help better develop his gross motor skills. It served the terrific secondary purpose of giving him more options on the playground as to what he could do during recess.

※ In addition, one of the older ED students helped Jerry during instruction time in the resource room. This particular child was very computer literate and showed Jerry how to use some of the programs that the other students in his class were familiar with. Jerry would snuggle up to this student and listened patiently. Whenever the ED student saw Jerry around the school he made a special effort to interact with him in the hallways. This relationship became an important one for Jerry and continued to some degree into the following year.

※ Another approach that worked well for us involved having the speech and language therapist come into the grade level classroom where she engaged Jerry in interacting with another student following a script. The script was usually a question that Jerry needed to ask (e.g., "What are you having for lunch?"), and how to wait for the other child to respond. Before involving the other student she rehearsed with Jerry the question he had to ask (of another child) in the speech and language classroom. When in the large group the question was written on a small whiteboard and she helped him read it to a peer volunteer. As Jerry built a small

We found two older boys who were willing to mentor and help Jerry and he responded to them immediately.

BRIGHT IDEA!

The speech and language therapist came into the regular classroom where she engaged Jerry in interacting with another student following a script.

repertoire of questions and practiced them, with minimal prompting he was starting to ask his peers the questions and responding to their attempts to interact with him. That made it easier for him to practice the real life experiences covered in the script, which were designed to help him not only to ask question but to appropriately respond to those posed by his classmates.

External Stimuli

❋ The OT staff taught Maria's parents and the teaching staff how to use a "Brush" to help her neurological system become more organized. (Brushing consisted of using a soft body scrub brush and a learned technique of scrubbing Maria's legs and arms as an attempt to help organize her neurological system.) This was done in a room where there were no other students and she did seem to benefit, at least briefly, to the brushing sessions. The winter in our part of the country can string day after day together where the entire student body is kept inside for extended periods. Maria was always a sort of "people barometer" and was strongly affected by the moods of those around her. When energy levels were high, she had a hard time focusing on her own tasks. The brushing helped to ease some of her anxieties.

Work Habits

Winter was also a point in the school year when we began expecting the students to become more independent in their work habits.

> By this time, Charlie was in the general education classroom for a good part of the day without either an aide or the special education teacher.

By this time, Charlie was in the general education classroom for a good part of the day without either an aide or the special education teacher. He had learned the rudiments of advocating for himself and would ask, when he needed, to receive additional instruction in the resource room. If someone was there this option was always granted. By the end of the year he was able to call the room himself to find out if he could get extra help.

> By the end of the year he was able to call the resource room himself to find out if he could get extra help.

When students have a one-on-one EA they can become too dependent upon that person, and especially if they have limited expressive language. It's therefore often easier for other students to talk to the special education child through the aide because they also rely on language to cue them. Our task was to begin to find ways to help the aides cue the students to talk directly to the child rather than ask the aide. Sometimes it was difficult for the aide not to jump in and answer or automatically respond to a classmate's inquiry because she wanted to be helpful. When we cotaught, the aides were often not in the room. Instead they were in another room to work with other children in a inclusion setting or were preparing materials to be used for academic instruction.

✹ Although Maria adored her EA, we wanted her to develop some independence. It put us in the awkward, but necessary position of having to wedge a bit of a crack into an otherwise wonderful and supportive relationship.

We looked at the assignments which Maria was able to do independently and informed her that she had to start to work on her own. In tandem, we set up a system by which Maria was reinforced for working by herself and we sent a daily note home to her parents attached to assignments she'd managed to complete with minimal help.

We discussed a method with her EA for her gradual fade from Maria's body space: First, she simply pushed her chair back a few inches at a time and eventually she was able to start walking around the room and helping others. This was all done at a snail's pace to downplay any sense of abandonment on Maria's part.

We also began reinforcing Maria for raising her hand rather than calling out when she needed teacher assistance. The more we worked at it, the more Maria learned to be proud and pleased by her own efforts, and everyone benefited as we sought to give her more space.

> We set up a system by which Maria was reinforced for working by herself and we sent a daily note home to her parents attached to assignments she'd managed to complete with minimal help.
>
> **BRIGHT IDEA!**

✹ At the end of each day the students had a homework book that they were required to complete. The children were asked to fill in the date, write down any assignments and then write sentences about what happened that day. Jerry became very attached to this routine. If he forgot his homework book he would become upset, sometimes to the extent that he would need to leave the classroom.

So we had to carefully structure this routine for him. He was asked to verbalize the assignment, while an EA or one of us wrote what he said, and then he was required to trace over what had been written. Under the student's written assignment longer notes were written by the teachers to help explain how to do the homework that was assigned as well as important future projects or class activities.

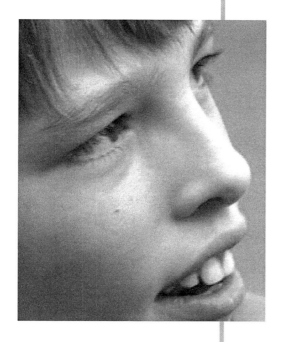

As the children left the room they were asked to tell "a good thing that happened that day," Eye contact was expected and the student could choose a "high five or hug." Jerry's EA rehearsed what he would say everyday. And some days he surprised us all and gave an answer that had not been practiced ahead of time. When this would happen, Jerry's famous grin would spread across his face like a crack on an iced-over lake.

(Note: pgs. 161–165 are reproducibles. They include: reading response sheet, a six-square form and an assignment adjustment form.)

Reading Response Sheet

Name _____ Date _____

Title; _____

Author: _____

```
┌─────────────────────────────────────────────────────────┐
│                                                         │
│                                                         │
│                                                         │
│                                                         │
│                                                         │
│                                                         │
│                                                         │
│                                                         │
│                                                         │
│                                                         │
└─────────────────────────────────────────────────────────┘
```

What was the setting? _____

Who are the main characters? _____

_____

Write events in order. (3) _____

_____

_____

What was your favorite part? _____

_____

I rate this book _____ stars. ☆☆☆☆

Six-Square Form

1. Before reading the picture book: predict what the book will be about by looking at the cover of the book.

2. Before reading: Divide the section into as many spaces as needed (two or four). Write a new vocabulary word in each section. (Have students explain with words and/or picture what the words mean to them.
Word ideas: cellar wilderness
handkerchief corncob pipe

3. While reading: Stop at a point in the book when you can make a prediction. Write the prediction before you turn the page for the answer.

4. After reading: draw a picture or write a sentence about a memory of something you've done and remembered when reading this book.

5. After reading: identify the book's setting and main characters.

6. After reading: rate this book (1–4 stars). Explain your rating: I liked this book because. . . Or, this wasn't my favorite book because. . .
☆☆☆☆

7. Write your name here _____
Evaluate your work (1–4 stars).
☆☆☆

Assignment Adjustments

Student's Name_____ Birthdate _____

1. This assignment was modified by: _____

2. How this assignment was modified: _____

_____

_____

_____

_____

_____

The attached assignment was adjusted from the original requirements that were expected. The assignment may have been shortened, read to a student, or the finished product may have been completed in a different format (e.g., picture drawn instead of written sentences, dictated and entered on a computer instead of hand written, etc.)

Chapter Eight

Winter Conferences

Once again the students are asked to come and to share their conference materials with their families. The winter conferences are conducted in the same manner as in the fall. The parents are sent information and by this time there has been enough communication between the families and the school staff so that there is a more comfortable level of exchange than at the start of the year. The students tend to understand their role in this conference better than the fall one because of the many interactions that have taken place in the classroom and the communications with parents via homework folders or phone calls which occur over the winter trimester. At this conference not only is there a review of progress but parents start to inquire about next year's placements (e.g., which teacher they will have, etc.). We also discuss ways to modify the spring curriculum for better academic success and often the families have questions about summer programs which are available for their children.

Academics—Reading

※ As the year progresses the major academic concern among most parents is still reading, since it is critical to so many other academic skill areas. Charlie's mother was shown the different comprehension strategies we had been using (e.g., the six-square form) and an explanation of each methodology was presented to her. In addition, we discussed a reading incentive program that had been established school wide and in which Charlie had really wanted to participate, mostly because he saw the other children getting prizes for taking part. Charlie's mother sighed that it was not easy to get him to do his homework, and especially to get him to read. We suggested that the reading times last only fifteen minutes and be divided between the two of them. Charlie would read part of the time and his mother would read to him as well. The entire time would then be credited to Charlie and he would rack up minutes for the incentive prizes currently being handed out to the student body.

※ Charlie's mother tried to work with him on any homework assignments and she asked if books from class readings could be put into his pack so that she could reinforce the

story ideas at home as part of the nightly reading sessions. She thought that if he had stories that he was familiar with, he might not be so resistant to a short reading time. Everyone marveled at the energy this mother put forth to help him learn. We also gave her recent brochures that the local public library had sent to the school about a reading program it was sponsoring for the summer. Charlie's mother was a working single mom and she needed to find reading programs which were helpful and could work around her schedule.

※ She had carefully filed all of the social stories which went home and would bring them out not only to encourage Charlie to read but also to review the social skills addressed in each book.

※ For Maria, a nightly reading program, which had been suggested at the fall conference was continued and modified slightly so she could practice her skills at home. We did not so much desire her parents to teach her reading but to reinforce the habit of reading so as to take pride in what she had learned. We set it up so Maria could check out a book from her reading box and could keep the book at home until she was done with it. Maria brought back the book along with a signed reading slip and checked out a new book to take home. (Maria was also able to use these slips for the school wide reading incentive program.) Maria was not overly thrilled with having to read but she was excited about getting "prizes" as part of the school sponsored reading program.

※ A similar program was designed for Jerry, except he was given the story he had recently read in the classroom. A short homework time for Jerry consisted of materials that he was familiar with and could feel successful completing at home. Jerry's parents participated in an after-school academic program to enhance his academic skills. All three sets of parents did as much homework follow-up as was possible each night, which was of invaluable assistance to us.

Social Skills

※ With the help of social stories, adult monitoring of behavior, and reinforcing Jerry's compliance (as opposed to his darting behavior) by this point in the school year all three students were able to walk the hallways independently using their hall passes. (Jerry had an adult shadow him at a distance for

Jerry and Maria needed supervision in the lunchroom because it was difficult for them to manage the noise and confusion. We presented the supervision to their parents as a preventive measure rather than a disciplinary tactic.

BRIGHT IDEA!

safety reasons, but he was extremely proud of himself when he could go from one classroom to another without having an adult walk beside him.)

⁂ The playground still presented some problems, but giving Jerry and Maria the option of an indoor recess helped. Neither student was fond of the cold, and supervised indoor recesses allowed them to interact with other children.

⁂ As mentioned earlier, part of the winter conferences was designed to talk about preparing the children to end the current school year successfully and to develop skills which would benefit them the following year. Charlie was not very organized and he was beginning to strike out at times on the playground and on the bus. Between us (including his mother) it was decided to start a home school communications notebook which would include both academic and social behavior as well as having his homework stapled into it so that his mother could find everything she needed in one place. If necessary, it allowed her to communicate to us problems that Charlie was having so the staff could change his routine.

⁂ For a short time additional supervision was put on the playground to assist Charlie so that he felt more comfortable and as a preventive measure to keep him from becoming so frustrated that he hit a classmate.

⁂ By this time, their cafeteria behavior had shown improvement, but both staff and parents thought Jerry and Maria needed to continue supervision in the lunchroom because it was difficult on certain days for them to mange the noise and confusion. We presented the supervision to their parents as a preventive measure rather than a disciplinary tactic.

⁂ Maria's involvement in a Circle of Friends group had helped reduce some of her aggression on the playground and she was able to go to the after-school daycare without adult supervision. Maria's parents decide to enroll her in the summer daycare program because they felt she needed social interaction with other children as much as academic instruction. A release of information was signed to allow the school staff to talk to daycare staff and set up a schedule that would enable Maria to attend it all summer.

> At this point in the school year all three students were able to walk the hallways independently using their hall passes.

> Charlie's mother was a working single woman and needed to find reading programs she could fit into her schedule.

Writing a Situation Specific Social Story

Charlie's mother told us that he loved to visit his grandparents, but did not respond well to having to take the trip. Family outings were also a problem because Charlie didn't like changes in his environment. Whenever he was on a bus or in the car on the way to a destination, he could become agitated and would say unbecoming statements to passengers on the bus or customers at a gas station, such as "You're fat." We suggested that she make a list of behaviors, which were expected of Charlie and we would help her write a social story about traveling to her parent's house. If she stuck to the two-week schedule and had him read the story two weeks before the trip it might help to prepare him. We decided that if Charlie drew the pictures it might also reinforce what she was trying to teach him. Listening to music on the school bus helped Charlie tolerate field trips and we suggested that she try a Walkman as well as the social story to help calm him when traveling in the car. A list of items (such as chewable candy) for a car survival box was another way for Charlie to help relieve some of this agitation.

In addition, the therapeutic riding lessons had proven successful and provided Maria with something to talk about that was positive and unique in her private life. Her parents were enthusiastic about the program and wanted to send her to the riding school throughout the summer.

⁜ As mentioned, the transition to the next grade level was already a top priority on these parent's list of concerns and it was something that we discussed at length with them. Maria's aggressive behavior had declined significantly, but she continued to struggle with social situations and with external stimuli.

⁜ During this conference, we discussed the possibility of our district employing a part-time consultant with expertise in the area of autism to observe Maria and Jerry and give us additional suggestions for improving our programming. In particular, we wanted to make the last trimester more productive.

For example, she recommended increased sensory breaks for Jerry as well as more "heavy work." The latter involves, for instance, having him carry books to the library and occasionally wearing weighted vests and weights around his ankles and arms for his "power walks." The exercise and "work" involved in these activities present Jerry with a stress reliever that proved very effective. As for the former, we also increased his sensory breaks and would essentially take them whenever we could tell he was becoming stressed. Both strategies improved our efforts with Jerry.

In addition, she demonstrated ways to escort him out of the room when he was having difficulties so staff wasn't put in a physically dangerous situation. Jerry's parents were also anxious for him to develop behaviors that would enable him to stay as included as possible.

In regard to Maria, the consultant taught us how to teach her the fundamentals of engaging in imaginary play, which was something she didn't understand. Maria's EA brought in a dollhouse, and following the consultant's suggestions we walked her through it with puppets so she had an opportunity to learn to play the way other children did.

Also, she provided us with "out of the box" ideas for adaptations to to enable Maria to develop skills necessary for a successful inclusion into the next grade. After the consultant's visit, Maria's and Jerry's parents were invited to a meeting where her recommendations were made.

 ※ Jerry's parents wanted to send him to a summer school class and were anxious that a one-on-one individual EA could be available to assist. February may seem a long way from June but in our district we had to start summer planning in order for special requests to be honored. We needed to have this information in order to follow the paper trail.

 ※ As with the fall conferences the IEP staff tried to have the families leave feeling that their child had made some progress and that some of their concerns would be addressed in the spring trimester.

(Note: pgs. 173–177 are reproducibles. They include: several suggested winter conference forms.)

Maria's consultant taught us how to show her the fundamentals of imaginary play, something she didn't understand. Maria's EA brought in a dollhouse, and we walked her through it with puppets. It gave her an opportunity to learn to play the way other children did.

BRIGHT IDEA!

Winter Conference

Conference dates are coming up soon in February. As in the fall, the children are expected to come and be a part of the conferences. They will once again share work and their self-assessment. I will again go through the school district's report card.

As a reminder, please enter the room as soon as you arrive. If I am finishing with the previous conference, please ask your child to begin sharing work in the back of the room. Due to a very tight schedule, we will have to stay on the twenty minute time schedule. If additional time is required, I will gladly set up another time to conference either on the phone or in the classroom. Thank you for respecting the schedules of the other families involved.

In addition to reviewing the social skills and work/study habits of your child, we will be discussing the academic progress relating to _____ District's _____ grade curriculum.

Language Arts

※ **Verbally shares information**
The children were asked to give a book talk of a favorite book during Children's Book Week. This talk was assessed.

※ **Comprehends an oral presentation**
The class listened to a short video segment about rocks and was then assessed.

※ **Applies reading strategies**
The children were asked to read a 100-word passage that is at a 2.5 reading level. I completed a running record with each child.

※ **Comprehends reading selections**
The children have been asked to complete story webs and to answer comprehension questions from selected readings. Their work will be shared at conferences.

※ **Expresses ideas clearly in writing**
Creative writing pieces have been assessed using the district's writing rubric. Frequency spelling words have also been retested. The assessments will be shared at conferences.

※ **Completes a graphic organizer**
Three separate graphic organizers have been completed by the class as a group project. At this time the children have not been required to independently complete a graphic organizer.

❋ Compose an informal letter

The children have been given additional opportunities to write an informal letter. Each student wrote a letter to Mr. Flanigan to thank him for the free book. This letter was assessed and the results will be shared at conferences.

Mathematics

❋ Place value

This outcome has been assessed. You may review your child's test at the conference.

❋ Basic facts to 18

We continue to work on math facts and give timed tests approximately three times each week. Each child has again been given the district's math facts assessments. Results will be recorded on the report card.

❋ Solves addition and subtraction story problems

We continue to work on solving verbal and written story problems. This outcome has not been assessed at this time.

❋ Tells time

We continue to work on problems relating to telling time. This outcome has not been assessed at this time.

❋ Recognized the value of coins

We have been working on problems with money. The goal is to have this outcome assessed by the time of conferences.

❋ Measurement

We continue to use the various forms of measurement in "real-life" situations in the classroom. This outcome has not been assessed at this time.

❋ Bar Graphs

We have worked on many graphs. This outcome has been assessed and the results will be shared at conference time.

❋ Calculators

We continue to use calculators in the classroom. If retesting was needed, this has been completed and results will be shared at conference time.

Science

⚹ **Classifies and describes rocks**

Our rock unit has been completed and assessed. The results will be shared at conference time.

⚹ **Classifies and describes rocks**

Our rock unit has been completed and assessed. The results will be shared at conference time.

⚹ **Weather**

We continue to work on our weather unit. The outcome has not been assessed at this time.

⚹ **Healthy body**

This unit is in progress. The goal is to have the assessment completed by conference time.

⚹ **Environment**

We continue to study the environment. This outcome has not been assessed at this time.

Social Studies

⚹ **Plan for personal growth**

We continue to do the self-assessments and set goals for the next trimester. These will both be shared at conferences.

⚹ **Compares various family cultures**

This unit is in progress. It will not be assessed by conference time.

⚹ **Investigate prominent Americans**

This unit continues to be in progress. It will not be assessed by conference time.

⚹ **Map skills**

This unit has been completed. The assessment has been given and will be shared at conference time.

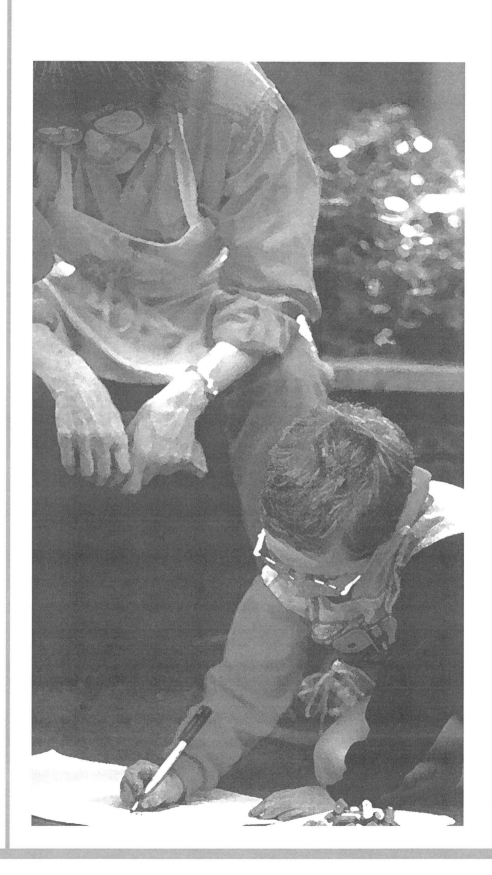

Chapter Nine

Spring

As snowdrops lose their flowers and daffodils start to sprout, a sense of renewed energy rushes through the school building each spring.

By this time, Charlie, Maria, and Jerry were pretty much content with their routine and felt comfortable in a classroom that six months ago was a foreign country. One of our most treasured achievements was that the other students in class had learned how to interact with them. Some students, in fact, were able to conduct very appropriate interactions and were capable of guiding our students with autism without infantilizing them. Maria had managed to become part of a small group of girls who were eager to have her join in their jump rope and other spring games. Her relationships had become solid enough that she no longer had to have constant playground supervision. Planning had become easier because the three were now able to do the daily routines.

Reading

By this time our three included students, who were by now able to read most of the second grade stories, were also ready to have their small group instruction times increased. This was done several different ways:

* Both Maria and Charlie arrived at school early. This allowed them to spend badly needed extra time in the resource room reviewing the easier, building-blocks concepts on the whiteboard or listening to a story which was being read.

* Group instruction was given in the larger class and independent work was completed in a small group. (*Note: IEPs need to be written in a way that allows for this flexibility. In addition, parents need to be aware of the reasons behind the flexible approach and why we pursue it.*)

* The weekly one-on-one reading with Debbie continued and was really starting to pay off.

* Our speech and language person considered Charlie to be a good candidate for the summer "Fast ForWord" Program. (See box at right.)

Because of the Circle of Friends, Maria had managed to become part of a small group of girls who were eager to have her join in their jump rope and other spring games.

(This is a comprehensive software program that provides phonemic instruction and requires trained specialists to administer it.)

※ Whenever possible, stories with next year's grade level themes were read so the children could have some background knowledge before entering that grade. For example, the next grade level reading curriculum has a unit on fairy tales. We used The Wright Group books (see box at left) and other easy-to-read materials out of the IMC to read to the students during a leisure time. Charlie enjoyed having these books on tape. Rainy spring recesses were spent listening to the tapes.

Written Language

With continued feedback from their parents, student writing skills continued to improve throughout the trimester.

※ Sentence strips were sent home for students to work on for punctuation errors.

※ In the homework notebooks, the parents continued to write ideas about the weekend news assignments or offered suggestions on how to do other kinds of writing. Since writing is such a challenging subject for all students at this age, not to mention those with language deficits, we have always felt strongly that our students wouldn't have made the progress they did without home support. We often remark to each other how lucky we were to have families who were so involved.

For example: Our class has a teddy bear—Cocoa—who "enjoys" spending a weekend with each child. At the end of the weekend the student is expected to write a story relating the activities of the past weekend to the class. Maria and her family participated in this activity. By this time of the year she was very familiar with the routine with the bear. Maria returned the bear and her story (in the form of a letter with which her family helped her) on Monday morning. She sat with the classroom teacher and held Cocoa as the teacher read the letter to the class. Debbie asked simple questions, giving Maria the opportunity to take part in the presentation. Everyone enjoyed hearing about Cocoa's adventures with Maria.

※ With practice at home as well as daily drills in school, Charlie could do the daily editing of sentences independently. At times he needed assistance to find the higher level skills such as the correct use of pronouns.

※ Jerry could now write a simple sentence staring with "I___," and his parents asked for the procedure so that a tutor could help him at home.

Spelling

Spelling continued to be a struggle for these students. In order not to discourage their efforts at learning, the spelling lists were modified to include only three to five words a week. Each student had their own dictated sentences to write with the target spelling word in the sentences. The same sentences were practiced everyday. This allowed Jerry an opportunity to finally start writing sentences that did not begin with "I." All of the sentences were about things the students could relate to.

Mathematics

To some degree all the students could give an answer to simple math sentences. For example, 6 + 4 =___. Charlie and Maria were able to memorize some addition facts and Maria understood the concept of adding on. Concepts such as telling time and fractions were more challenging. A variety of materials were used to help them with these concepts.

※ Charlie used small face clocks and fraction pieces, which went over the face of the clock. He needed individual attention from one of the teachers in order to complete telling time tasks.

※ Additional support was given to help Charlie understand the concept of what time daily routines took place (e.g., when he got up in the morning, what time school started, when the class went to lunch, what time school ended and when he went to bed).

Daily times often eluded him but he did begin to understand why it was important to learn this skill.

※ Small clocks were added to Maria's schedule so that she also could begin to make the connection to telling time. When an activity was completed she not only had to look at her clock but also the classroom clock in order to generalize the skill. By the end of the year Maria could tell time to the hour and with prompting could read the times on her individual clocks.

In order not to discourage their efforts, spelling lists were modified to only include three to five words a week and all sentences were about things the students could relate to.

BRIGHT IDEA!

Technology Skills

The computer can be a powerful tool for instruction when students become familiar with how to use it.

❋ Charlie was a devoted computer user. He preferred to use the keyboard for his sentences rather than to write them by hand. His mother made special arrangements for him to attend a computer lab class after school.

❋ Although a devoted OT therapist would go into the computer lab to help Maria use the keyboard correctly, she was much older before she appreciated computer programs. However, she did learn some basic computer skills which she surprised us with at a later time in her school life. With children with autism, it's often difficult to determine how much they're learning, because of the frequently disrupted feedback loop. For this reason, it's a good practice to always assume they're taking in more than you think at the time. With this in mind, Maria taught us all to be persistent in our efforts to teach her.

❋ Jerry had always been fascinated by the computer but struggled in learning how to use it at the beginning of the year. His older student mentor (the ED student mentor mentioned previously) assisted with this, and Jerry also learned by watching the other students. His skills improved and he actually enjoyed accomplishing academic tasks using the programs.

Social Studies/Science

One of our year-long science units involved the study of trees. We were fortunate to have a beautiful arboretum outside our classroom windows. The class studied and observed the many varieties of trees throughout the year. In spring each student plants a tree with the assistance of the high school ecology group.

❋ Charlie always had a marked aversion to getting his hands dirty and consistently resisted such typical, grade-appropriate activities as finger painting and gluing. So, we weren't sure how he would feel about digging in the dirt to plant a tree, which predictably would involve finding worms and having water spilled on his pants and shoes. All of these side effects tended to occur when elementary school students planted trees. For this reason, we used foreshadowing prior to the planting, attempting to anticipate everything that could happen. When planting day arrived, Charlie was given

Because of their disrupted feedback loop, it's often difficult to determine how much children with autism are learning. It's a good practice to assume they're taking in more than you think.

BRIGHT IDEA!

the opportunity to pick a partner from the class, and they were paired up with a high school student. Charlie sailed through the activity with barely a negative reaction and his tree—which he insists on visiting with his mother from time to time—is still growing fast, straight and tall.

✻ We also prepared Maria and Jerry the same way, but mostly because we didn't want them to be conspicuously paired with the EAs. Maria became so enthusiastic that she planted more than one tree.

Sensory Needs

✻ Weather permitting we began to take power walks outside the building.

✻ As a constructive way to calm restless bodies the students were asked to help to fill the bird feeders in the arboretum and to pull some of the weeds.

✻ The PT staff began to teach some of the students how to roller skate as another physical activity they could do to direct their nervous system.

✻ Jerry continued experiencing a more difficult time transitioning from the bus ride to the large classroom. So we continued to have him begin his morning in the special education classroom until he felt calm and could go to his included classroom. There were many days he required extra time on the therapy ball after coming to school. On these days the morning routine was done in the resource room. Planning at times was from minute to minute rather than day to day. As stated, you need to build in flexibility with students with autism in regard to their scheduling because while their good days are very good, the same can be said about their bad days.

✻ On his desk in the larger classroom Jerry had a picture card that showed different emotions. After the emotions were read to him, he would place a Velcro circle around the one he felt. This gave us a clue as to how to make him more comfortable, and whether or not he needed to have a sensory break before starting the next assignment.

✻ When they were restless and needed to be moving about, we gave them errands to do. For example, assigning them to carry large stacks of books to the IMC. This is comparable to heavy work and serves several purposes:

> As a constructive way to calm restless bodies, the students were asked to help to fill the bird feeders in our arboretum and to pull some of the weeds.

> When scheduling for students with autism, you need to build in flexibility, because while their good days are very good, the same can be said about their bad days.

Jerry had a picture card that showed different emotions. After the emotions were read to him he would place a Velcro circle around the one he felt.

This told us whether or not he needed to have a sensory break before starting the next assignment.

- it gives them a chance to move about when restless

- provides the advantages of heavy work

- and allows them to feel proud about their contribution to the class.

✳ Jerry's aggressive behavior was increasing and he was becoming more unpredictable when in the larger group. Aggressions directed toward his educational assistant and peers, not to mention himself, became more frequent. To ensure the safety and educational needs of the rest of the students, we were frequently faced with pulling Jerry from the classroom. He would then be given modified assignments to be completed in the resource room. Communication between all members of Jerry's educational staff took place daily. As previously mentioned, Jerry's program needed to have the flexibility to shift at a moment's notice. We requested a consultant who was an expert in behavior management to come into the school and help us develop a program that would reduce his aggressive behaviors so he would be able to transition as smoothly as possible to the next grade level.

It's not an easy task to find a consultant who not only knows how to teach students with autism, but also know something about the specific child. Fortunately, our district had several people who were hired for consulting and one had been working off and on with Jerry since he was in the early childhood program. A consultant has to not only observe but interact with the student. (This is exactly where many were inadequate: Beware of "expert consultants" who are incapable of conducting routine interactions with challenging students.) Suggestions need to be made in a helpful manner rather than a confrontational fashion. Suggestions for Jerry included more sensory breaks such as swimming, longer power walks and changing his program to include community outings.

As mentioned, the same consultant observed Maria and suggested that we find more responsible roles for her, since she so enjoyed helping others. We also increased the ways for her to practice interacting with others using puppets and partner computer programs.

Work Habits

While in the classroom, Maria's EA continued the fading process by giving her more "space" more frequently and for longer periods of time. The rest of the children in the class had become comfortable with having multiple adults in the classroom and were accustomed to the additional activity that was involved. We certainly felt fortunate to have extra helpers in the room, and when possible they helped the other students as well.

Beware of "expert consultants" who are incapable of conducting routine interactions and behavioral interventions with challenging students.

Chapter 10

Communicating with Educational Assistants

There are many books and pamphlets that discuss the role of the EA in an inclusion classroom setting. (See references, pg. 209.) Since EAs are a major cornerstone for many special education programs, it's helpful to have a clear source of data about the role and duties of an EA among a teacher's resource materials. Here, we've added specific procedures that have worked in our program with the hope that some of them will benefit you. Most of our suggestions are about EAs who are assigned to a single child but they can also be expanded for program EAs.

Going along with our philosophy that it takes a whole school to educate a child; the educational assistant is a key person who can help to make your special education program more successful. When working with EAs it's important to respect their expertise and to incorporate them into your team so they feel part of the educational process. When teachers respect their EAs the children sense it and see the EA as someone who can help them learn. When they don't respect their EAs, it erodes their credibility with the students and weakens what should be a strong part of your programming.

Many students with autism or pervasive developmental delay have one-on-one educational assistants or at least a program EA to help educate the child. Educational assistants come under many different titles whether they are called aides, educational assistants or paraprofessionals, and they usually don't have degrees in teaching. Some districts have a training program for EAs, but with the current crunch on school budgets, many districts rely on the teaching staff to do the inservicing.

The role of an EA needs to be explained. It often includes reinforcing of skills and at times reteaching specific academic skills. The job may also consist of some personal care, supervision on the playground and in the cafeteria, escorting students down the hallways, riding buses, learning how to observe sensory needs and communicating student behavior to the teaching staff. And these complex skills and duties are being requested of people who've likely had no previous training and

EXCELLENT
PRODUCT
ALERT!

"An Essential Guide for the Paraprofessional,"

**Peytral Publications
952-949-8707**

Have new EAs shadow a highly regarded teacher to observe how she interacts with the students.

BRIGHT IDEA!

Sensitive information about students with disabilities is not to be discussed at one's bowling league night, at church group, a neighborhood gathering, or over lunch during the school day.

probably haven't worked in a public school system with challenging children. It can be overwhelming at first. In addition, schools are notorious for skimping on inservices for educational assistants.

Training

Before the EA meets the student, it's important to supply her with as much information about children with autism as possible and detailed data about the specific child or children she will be working with. This needs to be done without the student present, and include parents if the EA is going to be a one-on-one assistant. The information, which has been gathered to help parents is also helpful for the EA to read or view. We have found it beneficial to have the EA read an outline describing major characteristics of children with autism and how they may differ from other students. Instructional videos can provide a quick overview of the kind of student the EA is expected to help instruct. Being teachers, our philosophy has always been that individuals can respond more intelligently when they have more information about a situation.

Try to establish an understanding that the role of the EA is to help a child with unique educational, social, and neurological needs. Have new EAs shadow a teacher to observe how she interacts with the student: The better the teacher, the better the modelling. Make sure the EA observes both the special and the general education teacher. If there is a capable EA in the building for your new EA to shadow, this is also recommended. To whatever extent you can, advocate for the district to send the EA to relevant workshops or conferences, because these provide invaluable background information. It also makes the statement that EAs are worthy members of your educational program. We make a point of sharing our conference experiences with EAs when we attend them.

As the EA develops a relationship with the child, students begin to communicate their own needs and the EAs gradually learn how to use that information.

The behavior intervention plan and IEP goals need to be shared with the EA so they can understand the specifics of the student's educational program. Along with this, make sure that from the beginning of your working relationship with the EA you communicate the need for confidentiality in regard to the students he will work with. Sensitive information is not to be discussed at one's bowling league night, at church group, a neighborhood gathering, or over lunch during the school day. We help our EAs rehearse what to say when confronted about sharing inappropriate information about any of our students in or out of school.

As mentioned, some students with autism tend to strike out. It is important that the assistant receive training from the OT/PT staff, a consultant, or teachers on how to safely (and with dignity) remove a student from the classroom to prevent her from striking out at others. If there is a behavior plan, the EA needs to know not only how to respond to inappropriate behavior but also those techniques which can redirect behavior and prevent "explosions."

Scheduling

Many of the children with autism and pervasive developmental delay have a one-on-one assistant. It's important to schedule times for the EA to do tasks other than that of being with the assigned child all day. The reason for this is that both general and special education teachers have to have time to interact with and teach the student. During these times, the EAs need something else to do. It's confusing for a child to have too many adults hovering over him (even if the schedule change is as simple as having the EA work with another child in the classroom while Debbie or Judi helps the student with autism).

In addition, we've found that occasionally having other individuals (for example, a different EA) work with the child helps prepare her for the day when the "regular" one-on-one EA is absent. And it benefits the EA to perform other duties and to teach other children, thus giving the EA a more global perspective on the school community as a whole. When we have been fortunate enough to have a program EA as well, that person also understands that she will be interacting with all the students in the program.

Allowing a one-on-one assistant to have other duties helps to prevent burn out. It has also been our experience that one-on-one EAs are very dedicated to that specific student. However there is a fine line between assisting and enabling. To prevent enabling from occurring, the EA needs to have other assigned duties, and as we just mentioned, this also gives the EA an opportunity to become acquainted with other children and staff members. In other words, don't set it up so the one-on-one EA is with that child all day long. (Note: When scheduling the EA for

> When helping, be discreet: It's confusing for a child to have too many adults hovering over him.

> Children with neurological difficulties can take a much longer time to comply with directions or provide an answer than other students. EAs need to be aware of individual learning styles so they can interpret the information and give the child time to respond.

other activities try to do it the same time every day and keep the number of people instructing the student to a minimal until the child learns to tolerate being around more individuals in the educational setting.)

It's important to find some time in your busy teaching schedule to talk to the EA about your program and the work she will be doing with your students. The EA will have many interesting observations and this is a time for her to state them, ask questions, and get information about upcoming academic skills that will be taught, modifications that may be needed and changes in routines such as assemblies or field trips. We have found that when an EA is part of the IEP team, he tends to conduct himself in a more professional manner, and is more closely connected to the goals and objectives for students he is working with.

Communicating Student Learning Style

In the days of internet access, interactive TV and a computer in virtually every home, daily life has picked-up its pace. Children with neurological difficulties sometimes take a much longer time to comply with directions or provide an answer than most people will tolerate. EAs need to be aware of individual student learning styles so that they can help interpret the information to the student and allow the child to respond.

How to talk to students

It's important to keep your language simple. That means talking in short complete sentences. Simple, clear statements, along with a waiting period allow the child to have an opportunity to respond appropriately. Giving directions one step at a time and waiting for the child to process each direction sets the student up for success at completing a certain task.

Remember that the other children in the classroom observe the adults for cues on how to approach and interact with the student with autism. The other students interact using what they see and hear the adult staff do. If the language is kept simple, and in complete sentences it helps prevent the other students from talking down or using "baby talk" when they get a chance to interact with the child with autism.

We have had an occasional problem with the volume new EAs use in the classroom. When instructing students, there often needs to be a lot of talking. The trick is to assist the student without distracting the other children and drawing attention to what is happening at the desk of the student with autism. This is one reason why it is important for teachers to initially model these interactions for EAs.

An EA needs to learn to be sensitive to the child's attempts to communicate either through language or body gestures. Working toward greater independence is always our goal. Often other children or adults will attempt to communicate to the child through the EA. The EA needs to feel comfortable telling these people to talk directly to the child rather than talking to her in the third person by having the EA "translate" everything.

When another person is attempting to speak with the student, it's important for the EA to model the correct response, and then give the child the opportunity to practice what has been modeled. The child needs to be praised for her efforts to respond to verbal communication. Try to have the EA find ways for the child to initiate her needs through conversation. Just like teaching academic skills the student with autism needs to learn the purpose for social communication. For example, when someone says "hi" to the child, the child needs to learn how to respond back.

Learning how to anticipate transitions

Teach the EA how to foreshadow transitions or changes in schedules and expectations. This is one reason why using a visual schedule can be helpful because it not only cues the student but also the EA, who can prepare the child that a transition is about to take place. Remember to praise the child for making a successful transition. Sometimes a simple 'thank you' is all that is needed.

Being aware of sensitivities

Knowing the sensitivities of the child to her environment is important. The EA must be aware of such factors as the lighting and noise levels, as well as other environmental issues at all time. Knowing this helps to direct the child where to stand or sit in a classroom, in a line, or how to tolerate noisier and more confusing environments such as the playground. Your area may have environmental issues that are unique—e.g., a school located beneath an airport flight path: It's important to do an informal but thorough inventory of the specifics of your setting.

Many children and some adults will attempt to communicate to the child through the EA.

The EA needs to feel comfortable telling these people to talk directly to the child rather than "translating" everything.

BRIGHT IDEA!

We help our EAs rehearse what to say when confronted about sharing inappropriate information about any of our students in or out of school.

BRIGHT IDEA!

Working toward independence

Once classroom routines and the relationship with the individual student become familiar it is important to find ways the EA can reinforce and develop more independence. Students gain independence more quickly when routines and teaching procedures remain consistent.

Unless there is a flight or security risk the student needs to learn how to walk in the hallway in a way that is age appropriate. That means, among other things, the EA should not be holding the child's hand. The student with autism has to learn the social rules like all of the other children, and when the EA is seen holding the child's hand it lowers everyone's expectations of that student's capabilities. When the class passes in the hallway we try to get the student to use the general education teacher and the children in front of her as models. The EA needs to walk behind the child, and when necessary verbally guide the student to follow the school rules for behavior in the hallways.

Using visual hallway passes—i.e., a picture cuing system—has helped the students with autism in our class learn to navigate the hallway by themselves with only spot monitoring of their behavior.

The EAs who are observant have been able to learn when to give the child with autism "space" to do some tasks independently. They move about the classroom during this time helping other children or assisting the teacher by correcting papers or setting up future projects. By doing this, they appear to be more of a working member of the classroom in the eyes of all the children and not just a "helper" for the student with autism. Before moving away from the student, the EA tells the child that she is doing her work well and that the EA is going to help another student or sit away from the desk until the student with autism needs help or is finished. Small moments of independent work help to build more autonomous behaviors. We have also found that children get tremendous satisfaction telling parents that they're able to complete work by themselves.

In summary, a sound working relationship between the EA and the rest of the IEP team can develop when the EA feels part of the team educating children in an inclusive setting.

Chapter Eleven
Communicating with Parents

As we have stated frequently throughout this book, proactive relationships with the parents of our students with autism is a top priority and we make every effort to make it happen. We start opening these lines of communication even before school begins each year and invite them to contact us at home, or make arrangements to meet them in school. Among other things, we want to learn what their vision is for their child and what they hope to see accomplished in the school year to come. And we wish to learn every detail they're willing to share about their child so we are able to approach each student in the most positive and productive way possible. Knowledge in this sense, is not only power, it's survival.

In addition, we always try to empathize with the parent's views. Few people know better than teachers the daily struggles parents with children with autism face and how strong their need is to be advocates for their child. Once parents feel we are sincere in our intentions and that we are devoted to all our students, we begin to forge a positive and successful alliance.

These parents, of course, vary a great deal from one to another. Some possess a keen sense of humor, which serves to keep us going through difficult times. Others have done extensive research into their child's disability and have made heroic efforts to access as many services as they can. These types of parents are walking encyclopedias and can be a tremendous source of practical information for us, and we in turn have learned a great deal from them. Some suggestions for optimizing these vital relationships include:

※ Be unrelenting in your attempts to communicate with parents before the school year begins and problems develop, because this is a time when people are relaxed and sharing information with them guarantees the best possible chance of success.

※ Try to find out what times during their day your parents will be available for consultation and how they would like to

> Proactive relationships with parents of students with autism is a priority and we make every effort to make it happen. We start opening these lines of communication before school begins each year.

Try to find out what time during the day parents are available for consultation and how they would like to communicate.

BRIGHT IDEA!

When calling parents during a crisis time avoid saying things like, "Albert hit someone on the playground again!"

That's a setup for trouble, because it sets a negative tone for the information you're trying to relate and it gives a negative message about your feelings toward their child.

BRIGHT IDEA!

communicate. Make notes of these times somewhere so you don't lose them, because this will go a long way toward reducing friction in your alliance with them. Ask them for voice mail numbers, extension numbers and when possible, email addresses. The latter is often a good way to contact them without intruding into their daily schedules.

✻ It's extremely important that a system for crisis situations be established at the beginning of the year. And be aware that these are very delicate situations. When calling the parents during a crisis time avoid saying things like, "Albert hit someone on the playground again." That's a setup for trouble, because it sets a negative tone for the information you're trying to relate and it gives a negative message about your feelings toward their child. No parent likes to hear that and there's always a more positive way to state things. It's very hard not to jump directly to the problem when your own adrenaline is running high, but you must restrain yourself. Judi, as the parent of a child with severe learning disabilities took many such calls and knows personally how distressing that kind of contact can be. You can convey the same message by saying something like, "Mary, this is Judi, can I have a minute of your time. We have been delighted with Jimmy's progress this year and really appreciate your hard work in helping us put together a strong behavior management program. This has been a really great week for Jimmy, but today there was an incident on the playground that we need to discuss. We need your help in finding a way to keep this from happening. I've got a few ideas, but I'd really appreciate some suggestions from you too. Here's what we're thinking . . ."

✻ Remember that parents may be at work and they might need a few moments to find a private place to discuss the situation. It's better to start out by saying, "We need to call upon your support again, or we need your help in solving a problem." This will give parents a chance to switch from their current situation and focus on what is about to be discussed. Sometimes they may have to call back because they need to go to a more private place. If that's the case, be patient and give them the opportunity to do so. These things have to be handled very tactfully and the last thing you want to do is blurt out bad news quickly and impatiently without respect to their feelings. By enlisting their help, it cues the parents to the fact that this conversation is serious. Always thank them for their input. These simple, common courtesies will strengthen your alliance. Conversely, their absence can spell doom for your relationship.

✻ If parents are at work, don't ever tell a coworker why you are calling. Just give a message to have them call back a soon as possible. The coworker does not need to know that school staff is calling unless the parents themselves choose to tell them. That's their business.

✻ Give parents a call or note on days when something great has happened. They too often hear the problems and the negatives . . . they also need to hear successes. Like everyone else, they need to have reinforcement.

✻ It is also helpful for the students to write a note about their successes. Like most kids, children with autism enjoy telling their families about the good things they've done.

✻ We have found that parents are most interested in getting information which helps teach and educate their child. While this may seem obvious, it's important to always keep it in mind. Share articles, books, videos, and conference information that might be of value to them. Some parents are interested in support groups, others prefer to communicate only to school staff. Offer them options, but don't shove it down their throats. Some parents feel uncomfortable about talking in a support group.

✻ Someone in your building should have access to medical resources provided by physicians and psychologists who have an understanding of children with autism. Find out who these people are and cultivate a working relationship with them. It'll save you a lot of time and greatly enhance your success with these students, and will impress their parents. It's been our experience that parents are grateful for this information, especially if they are struggling with their current doctor.

✻ Try to hold additional meetings, which would allow the parents to attend. Also, invite parents to visit the classroom or volunteer at school. We have discovered that those families who come in to volunteer learn the workings of a general education classroom and have opportunities to interact with many children. One nonworking mother volunteered to be a mentor in our classroom after her son had moved to the next grade level. Her son did not need as much of her attention and she wanted to help another person's child.

Whatever you do, if parents are at work, don't tell their coworkers why you are calling. Just give a message to have them call back as soon as possible.

BRIGHT IDEA!

Give parents a call or note on days when something great has happened. They too often hear the problems and the negatives . . . they also need to hear successes.

BRIGHT IDEA!

- Try to find out who in your community can best serve as a consultant for the school staff and the parents. In spite of a person's best effort, some additional resources have to be called upon. We were fortunate to have a therapeutic riding school near our district that our parents frequently took advantage of, including Judi, whose daughter started as a student and advanced to an assistant riding instructor. If an outside consultant comes in to school, either schedule an informational meeting so parents can attend, or contact them by phone or mail.
- As we've said before, not every parent was thrilled with our teaching. When we were confronted by angry parents, it was often difficult to convince them our efforts were student-directed and in the best interest of their child. When we were second-guessed or constantly challenged we were always willing to explain our reasoning behind the methods being used. The trick is to be very professional. This is far easier said than done, because when you are trying hard to apply what you firmly believe are "best practices," negative feedback can be emotionally crushing even for the most hardened veteran teacher. Frankly, it's painful to realize at times that you're not trusted and valued as professional educators.
- Remember that even when parents are upset, the primary goal is to do your best job with their child. This goal cannot be lost and the child must never feel like he or she has been slighted. It's unfortunately a very human tendency to take our frustration out on the child or to subconsciously sabotage the educational program. Our goal has always been to provide the best possible education for every student we serve. Again, many of these things may seem obvious, but they are easy to forget under duress.

This is one of the best reasons for developing a list of parent support groups and other resources. Sometimes angry families need a place to vent frustrations. It's especially important to show your appreciation of good information that comes from these groups. Sometimes it's a long journey before parents become comfortable with the school environment. Try always to implement parent suggestions—when they are reasonable and reflect sound practice: That shows your willingness to participate in the child's development.

(editor's note: During the course of writing this book, we came into contact with Lee Wilder, a mother from Kentucky who had adopted two siblings with multiple severe disabilities, including one with autism. We hit it off, and after several conversations, decided her story would be a valuable addition to this chapter. It offers a poignant example of the obstacles many parents face, the will they exert, and the love they have that drives them to optimize opportunities for their children.)

One Family's Story

Dear Judi,

My husband and I were married in 1981 while living in New Orleans. In 1983 I lost the baby I was carrying and was told I would no longer be able to have children. This devastated both of us. Shortly thereafter, we had the chance to go to Saudi Arabia, where my husband, JD, served as a helicopter instructor and I was secretary to a senior military advisor. While there, I wrote over 800 letters to adoption agencies worldwide and we tried continually for seven years to adopt without success.

I returned to America the weekend of July 4, 1989, while JD stayed to complete his contract. In lieu of adoption, I became a foster parent and took in emergency placements, including siblings when the occasion arose. I was still working for the government, now in Yuma, Arizona. The child care facility was wonderful, allowing me to bring in my foster children at a moment's notice.

JD remained throughout Desert Storm and came home at the end of 1990. At the time, I had two children, a brother and sister in foster care, and we were told we could adopt them. JD fell in love with them as well, and we began going to Phoenix on day trips looking for a place to live. The children were excited about picking out their new rooms.

JD got a job in Phoenix, flying a medical helicopter. The day we were to move, Child Protective Services (CPS) decided we couldn't take the children out of town and removed them from our care. It tore our hearts out and it's hard to imagine what it must have done to the children.

Then, a second girl, 18 months old, came into our care. Again, we were elated and more than ready to start all over again. Her story, however, was a heartbreaker. She was born drug addicted and legally drunk. At the age of six months, she had been left unattended in a crib for four days, and at that point was taken into protective custody and put into foster care. CPS continued to work with the birth mother with the idea of returning the child to her, but she was unable or unwilling to keep the terms of her contract, including a provision to enter a drug rehab program.

We were to eventually discover the extent of her disabilities: Attention Deficit Hyperactivity Disorder (ADHD), Sleep Disorder and Seizure Disorder.

This lovely little girl arrived for placement one bright day with a garbage bag full of dirty clothes. When I looked at her my heart melted. However, JD, in his excitement to prepare a meal for us started a grease fire and we had to call the fire department. Though a momentary setback, this event was to provide a wonderful yield later.

That weekend her case worker paid a us visit and said as far as she was concerned the placement was final. It would be just a quick paper shuffle and she'd be ours. She added that we could begin thinking about a name, and we settled on Jayme Elizabeth.

Things went well during the next few weeks. Then CPS called again and said they had made a "terrible mistake." They had found another placement, which they thought more appropriate, and wanted Jayme back. We were stunned, but this time we weren't about to surrender without a fight.

During the next few weeks CPS haunted our home. There were numerous calls, threats, and intimidations and they parked across the street to take photos and followed whenever we would leave.

During one of their harassing calls, a contractor—who just happened to be repairing the damage from JD's stove fire—overheard and asked if he could help. He seemed an unlikely ally at first, but he was to provide our deliverance. He called a friend at the Phoenix American Civil Liberties Union, who put us in touch with an attorney and restored to us a measure of hope.

Recharged, we went back on the offensive, calling congressmen and senators and everyone else we could think of. We talked, fumed, cried and paced the floors, all the while afraid we were going to lose Jayme, too. Finally, we came home one Friday night and our answering machine

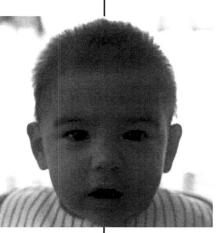

informed us we were scheduled for a meeting the following Monday, when we would have to give Jayme back to them.

For the next two days, we rocked Jayme to sleep fearing that if we put her down we would never hold her again. We arrived at our attorney's office Monday morning to find him pacing the floor. He told us we would have to turn her over in an hour.

Again, we took the offensive. We filed a suit in Federal Court for violation of our civil rights, and a Phoenix newspaper called to write an article. Then the TV stations starting calling. For the next 12 months we were on television and radio constantly. I've kept most of the tapes for posterity.

It took exactly one year to the date for us to legally adopt her. In the process, we changed Arizona's foster placement and adoption policies, including the addition of 13 new legal citings that encourage keeping siblings together.

That became significant, because when Jayme was three, her birth mother had another child. At the time, she had been walking the streets and turning tricks for drugs. Like Jayme, her brother was born legally drunk and drug addicted and had to spend the first three weeks of his life in detox.

When he was released, his grandmother took him home. One day soon after, the birth mother paid a visit, lifted her new baby off the ground, uttered a profanity, and threw him across the room. Since we'd encouraged Jayme's grandmother to maintain contact, she called us about the situation. As a result, I phoned CPS (briefly our ally) to help her keep her daughter away from her grandson.

Eventually, CPS removed him from the grandmother and placed him in Crisis Nursery. We then petitioned—partially under the new laws that resulted from our case with Jayme—to adopt her sib and were soon allowed to bring him home.

However, we soon realized there was something terribly wrong. I took him to our doctor, and three days after he'd arrived at our home, he was in the hospital dying. I was frantic and JD was pacing, but the baby survived. Before his second birthday, we made 12 visits to the hospital, 11 of which were in intensive care. At about this same time, we went to court and Erik officially became our new son.

Due to ongoing health issues, Erik slept in a crib in our bedroom for the first three years of his life. Each and every one of these nights, he woke up screaming. So we took him back to our doctor and began to collect diagnoses. First, they said he had a Level 4 Sleep Disorder, which meant he had night terrors and was unable to sleep through the night. From there we progressed to ADHD, then to Tourette's Syndrome, Sensory Integration Disorder, Tactile Defensive Disorder, and finally the one diagnosis that pretty much covers all of the above, Autism. In addition, he is nearsighted, and is currently being fitted for braces to be worn inside his shoes.

But it was the diagnosis of autism that was the final answer to all the questions we had about him. He has always marched to the beat of a different drummer, or as JD likes to say, "Erik leads his own 76-trombone band."

Today, so I can be on hand for their constant medical problems, I no longer work. Jayme has settled into a somewhat predictable cycle with her seizures, and I have learned to be able to see them coming ahead of time. Jayme, too, is beginning to recognize the symptoms. Lately, she has begun to show a disturbing amount of memory loss, often associated with seizures. This is of great concern, because she is only 10. It impacts on her school work and has been the subject of numerous IEP meetings to accommodate her special needs.

These days, I am constantly in touch with our school district, where I often volunteer, or try to obtain educational materials to help with my children's education. I spend considerable time searching the internet for help, go to the library for books and attend school all day with Erik when his aide is unavailable. I try to provide the classroom with needed items when I can, and work one-on-one with special needs children. I am constantly on the lookout for new ways to teach Erik and other children with autism, so I am on occasion able to educate the school in ways to help my child.

As with many children with autism, Erik is intelligent with a mind like a steel trap. He also demonstrates a keen sense of humor. When something tickles him, he will giggle and ask if you think it's funny too. I am concerned about his lack of social skills, and he's yet to learn the names of any children in his homeroom. He does, however, know one student in his resource room, "Jaime," because it's pronounced the same as his sister's.

It has been somewhat of a long road and we're nowhere near the end of our journey. But we wouldn't have changed a single day of it all, not even the lowest points. And I have to say, it's because of teachers and support staff—like those of you who are reading this book—that we hold out great hope for the future of our two children. Keep up your good work and thank you for listening to my story.

Sincerely,
Lee Wilder
Friday, Apr. 5, 2001

Appendix

Behavioral Intervention Plan (BIP)

(Note: All children who exhibit behaviors that disrupt the learning process need to have a BIP in place on their IEP. Not every state follows the same form. This is a sample of the kind of plan that is required in our state and may be helpful as a guideline for reducing inappropriate behavior and increasing more socially acceptable behavior.)

Behavioral Intervention Plan

Name: Maria   DOB: 4/30/93   Grade: 2nd   Date Developed: 2/15/01

I. Description and Definition of Behavior:

Maria's behavior, being addressed at this time, is physical aggression to adults and peers in the school environment.

"Physical aggression" is defined as any action that can inflict bodily harm to adults or peers. This includes, intimidating others by towering over peers and pushing with her body, hitting, kicking, punching, and throwing objects at others in a school environment.

A. Reason for Change:

This behavior is needed to change to ensure the safety of herself and others. Also, this change is needed to maintain a respectful and productive learning environment for all.

B. Frequency, Duration, and Intensity:

The physical aggression described has been documented since Maria has entered the _____ School system in the fall of 1998. She has demonstrated physical aggression (hitting, kicking, pushing and throwing objects) whenever she becomes frustrated or angry, when she appears to feel her body space has been invaded, or when she's confronted with a task which she finds too difficult to complete.

This behavior, which has intensity that can frighten or hurt peers and even adults, has been documented up to several times a day. Physically aggressive behavior has resulted in Maria being removed from a classroom, playground, or other places in the school building and escorted to the special education room where there is a space provided to calm her without further hurting others (and herself). To date, Maria has become physically aggressive towards staff and peers 33% of her days at school. These incidences consist of physical assaults on the playground (13 times), in the classroom (11 times), in the cafeteria (4 times), and in the hallways (5 times).

C. Identified Antecedents and Purpose of Behavior:

Behaviors identified above are most likely to manifest themselves when Maria is working with an adult and she is asked to make corrections, redo a task or start an assignment that strikes her as too difficult to complete.

These behaviors also occur when Maria feels that her body space has been invaded or when she is trying to get the attention of another person and seems unsure of how to do it in a more appropriate manner. Maria can also strike out and cry when there is a loud and unexpected noise.

The purpose for the aggressive behaviors seems to serve the function of avoiding tasks, an inability to resolve conflicts or communicate her needs, and an inability to manage unexpected environmental distractions in a more appropriate fashion.

II. Prevention Plan:

The following positive preventative techniques have proven to redirect physically aggressive behaviors as well as increase more desired behaviors.

- Praise all efforts on Maria's part to make self-initiated attempts to begin her assignments.

- Praise all self-initiated efforts to use the items in her sensory box in order to help her get through a difficult situation.

- Encourage Maria to write in her homework book or email to her family something she has done well that day.

- Use social stories to help Maria practice and understand more appropriate ways to manage her frustrations and gain peer attention.

- Encourage Maria to sit in a group or stand in line where she feels comfortable and praise her for using the designated spot.

- Whenever possible forewarn Maria about a fire or tornado drill so she can prepare herself for the loud noise.

- Give Maria a strategy to use during the ringing of the fire or tornado drills alarm. Holding her hands over her ears and telling herself that the sound will not harm her seems to work.

(Note: The sound may still be painful but she needs to know that it will not strike her and hurt her in that way.)

- Power walks through the hallways are necessary to reduce tension before school and during sensory breaks.

- Foreshadowing transitions either verbally or using her visual schedule is important to help prepare Maria for a change in routine.

- Before Maria starts to drink at the fountain tell her she needs to stop at the count of ten. This will prevent her from spending minutes at the fountain and a struggle to remove her from it.

- Provide a choice for where she can complete difficult work. (She can choose between her desk in the classroom, the work table in the hallway, the resource room or an acceptable alternative provided by Maria.)

- Have an alternative place for Maria to have a recess on days when she is struggling with her ability to stay calm.

- If possible give Maria a choice of the sequence for completing difficult tasks.

- If possible give Maria a choice on how to complete the tasks.

- State directions one at a time and praise effort for complying.

- Give a high five or thumbs up sign for appropriate behavior.

III. Intervention Plan:

When physical aggression occurs in the school environment, Maria will be given directions to go to the "mood change" area until she is able to calm down. She will be given the choice of leaving on her own or being escorted.

Redirection:

- Change the location for completing or modifying the required task.
- Take a sensory break or power walk.
- Break an assignment down and have her complete it in steps.
- Praise compliance.

De-escalation:

Teacher/staff behavior will remain calm and a nonthreatening tone will be used in response to inappropriate behavior. Consequences will be stated in a matter of fact manner. Maria will be given additional time and space to comply in situations which are not safety issues. Reinforce Maria's efforts to regain control of her anger and behave appropriately.

Protection/Crisis Plan:

When Maria becomes physically aggressive with objects or people trained staff needs to assist her to the special education area.

First, she will be asked to leave. If she refuses the crisis team will be called and she will be removed to an area designed to help her calm down before she can return to the classroom.

To prevent damage to personal or school property, when she is frustrated and angry, all materials will be removed from Maria's reach. When Maria has been removed because of physical aggression, per parent request she will call her mother/father to tell them.

IV. Evaluation:

The criteria for success will be the attainment of her IEP goal three (which is a behavioral goal, teaching appropriate ways to manage her frustration longer). The special education staff will document data on how many times the crisis intervention was needed and why. The system used to collect data will be in the form of a daily log consisting of incidence reports. This plan will be re-evaluated during each IEP review and changed accordingly.

V. Communication:

All IEP team members will receive a copy of this plan. Also, the building crisis team members will have a copy to assist the special education staff as needed, or if key special education people are unavailable to work directly with her. If contingency plans are needed, the current building crisis plan will be followed. Key special education staff working directly with Maria in conjunction with her parents will make emergency changes as needed.

References

Carle, Eric (1977). "The Grouchy Ladybug." Hong Kong: HarperCollins Publishers.

Carle, Eric (1987). "The Very Hungry Caterpillar." New York: Penguin Putman Books for Young Readers.

Cumine, Val, Leach, Julia, and Stevenson, Gill (1998). "Asperger Syndrome." London: David Fulton Publishers Ltd.

Gerland, Gunilla (1997). "Finding Out about Asperger's Syndrome, High Functioning Autism and PDD." London & Philadelphia: Jessica Kingsley Publisher.

Gray, Carol (2000). "The New Social Story Book." Arlington, TX: Future Horizons.

Hammeken, Peggy A. (1996). "An Essential Guide for the Paraprofessional." Minnetonka, MN: Peytral Publications.

Kiln, Aim, Ph.D. & Volkmar, M.D. (1996). "Asperger Syndrome: Treatment and Interventions, Some Guidelines for Parents. Learning Disabilities Association of America

Kinney, Tom (1998). "Straight Talk about Autism," a two video series. Verona, WI: Attainment Company.

Maurice, Catherine, editor, (1996). "Behavioral Interventions for Young Children with Autism." Austin, TX: Pro-Ed.

Maurice, Catherine (1993): "Let Me Hear Your Voice, A Family's Triumph over Autism." New York: Fawcett Columbine.

McKean, Thomas A. (1996) "Soon Will Come the Light." Arlington, TX: Future Horizons.

Myles, Brenda Smith & Simpson, Richard (1998). "Asperger Syndrome: A Guide for Educators and Parents." Austin, TX: Pro-Ed.

Sewell, Karen (1998). "Breakthroughs: How to Reach Students with Autism." Verona, WI: Attainment Company.

Waltz, Mitzi (1999). "Pervasive Developmental Disorders: Finding a Diagnosis and Getting Help." Sebastopol, CA: O'Reilly & Associates, Inc.

Wagstaff, Janiel (1994). "Phonics That Work! New Strategies for the Reading/Writing Classroom." Scholastic Professional Books

Winebrenner, Susan (1996). "Teaching Kids with Learning Difficulties in the Regular Classroom." Minneapolis, MN: Free Spirit Publications.